202 Lamb Chop and Cutlet Recipes

(202 Lamb Chop and Cutlet Recipes - Volume 1)

Maria Howard

Copyright: Published in the United States by Maria Howard/ © MARIA HOWARD

Published on August, 22 2020

All rights reserved. No part of this publication may be reproduced, stored in retrieval system, copied in any form or by any means, electronic, mechanical, photocopying, recording or otherwise transmitted without written permission from the publisher. Please do not participate in or encourage piracy of this material in any way. You must not circulate this book in any format. MARIA HOWARD does not control or direct users' actions and is not responsible for the information or content shared, harm and/or actions of the book readers.

In accordance with the U.S. Copyright Act of 1976, the scanning, uploading and electronic sharing of any part of this book without the permission of the publisher constitute unlawful piracy and theft of the author's intellectual property. If you would like to use material from the book (other than just simply for reviewing the book), prior permission must be obtained by contacting the author at author@smilecookbook.com

Thank you for your support of the author's rights.

Content

202 AWESOME LAMB CHOP AND CUTLET RECIPES 7

1. 17 Minute Spiced Lamb Cutlets With Couscous Salad Recipe 7
2. 5 Ingredient Dukkah Lamb Cutlets With Broccoli Rice 7
3. Asian Style Lamb With Watermelon Coriander Salad 8
4. BBQ Lamb Cutlets With Tomato Ginger Curry Sauce 8
5. Bacon Wrapped Lamb Cutlets With Beans And Fennel (gluten Free) 9
6. Baharat Lamb 9
7. Baked Five Spice Lamb Cutlets 10
8. Baked Lamb Chops With Fetta Crumble . 10
9. Baked Lamb Chops With Pumpkin 11
10. Balinese Lamb Chops 11
11. Barbecued Moroccan Lamb With Potatoes 12
12. Barbecued Lamb Chops With Romesco Sauce 12
13. Barbecued Lamb Cutlets With Fresh Mint Red Wine Vinegar Sauce 13
14. Barbecued Lamb Cutlets With Two Salsas 13
15. Barbecued Mint Lamb Chops With Charred Corn And Chilli Slaw 14
16. Barbecued Spiced Lamb Chops With Pumpkin Salad 14
17. Barbecued Tandoori Lamb Cutlets With Coconut Rice Recipe 15
18. Basil And Goat's Cheese Lamb Racks 16
19. Best Ever Grilled Lamb Chops With Lemon Myrtle Butter 16
20. Black Bean Lamb Cutlets With Roasted Spring Veggies 17
21. Braised Tomato Lamb Chops With Fetta. 17
22. Cajun Lamb With American Slaw And Corn 18
23. Char Grilled Lamb Chops With Greek Salad 18
24. Chargrilled Garlic And Pepper Lamb Chops With Mixed Bean Salad 19
25. Chargrilled Lemon And Rosemary Lamb Cutlets Recipe 19
26. Charred Lamb Chops With Greek Salad ... 19
27. Cheesy Cutlets With Avocado Dip 20
28. Chermoula Lamb Cutlets With Coconut Pilaf 21
29. Chermoula Lamb Cutlets With Dried Fruit Couscous 21
30. Chilli And Orange Lamb Chops With Pearl Couscous Salad 22
31. Chinese Lamb With Ginger Sauce 22
32. Chutney And Rosemary Lamb Chops 23
33. Classic Crumbed Cutlets 23
34. Coriander Lamb With Roasted Carrots And Quinoa 24
35. Costolette D'agnello 25
36. Crumbed Lamb Cutlets With Pasta Salad . 25
37. Crumbed Lamb Cutlets With Pumpkin Salad And Pesto 26
38. Crumbed Lamb Cutlets With Roast Greek Salad Vegetables 26
39. Crushed Peas And Potatoes With Sumac Lamb Cutlets 27
40. Cumin And Sesame Lamb With Silverbeet And Beetroot Salad 27
41. Cumin Lamb With Pumpkin Chickpea Pilaf 28
42. Curried Lamb Cutlets With Radish Yoghurt 29
43. Curried Lamb With Rice Pilaf 29
44. Dukkah Lamb Cutlets With Tomato And Spinach Salad 30
45. Dukkah Crusted Lamb Chops With Fruit And Nut Couscous 30
46. Easy Braised Lettuce And Peas With Lamb 31
47. Fennel And Chilli Spiced Lamb Chops With Superfood Vegetable Mix 32
48. Feta And Semi Dried Tomato Crusted Lamb 32
49. Fresh Minted Peas With Spring Lamb 33
50. Garlicky Lamb Chops With Barbecued Green Beans 33
51. Greek Lamb And Vegie Tray Bake 34
52. Greek Vegetable And Lamb Tray Bake 34
53. Green Masala Lamb Cutlets 35
54. Green Olive Lamb With White Bean Puree

55. Grilled Lamb Cutlets With Olives, Mint And White Bean Puree 36
56. Haloumi Lamb Cutlets With Greek Potato Parcels 37
57. Herb Crusted Lamb Cutlets With Tomato Chutney 37
58. Herb Crusted Lamb With Crisp Potatoes 38
59. Honey Sesame Lamb Cutlets 38
60. Indian Spiced Lamb Chops With Curried Spinach And Currant Pilaf 39
61. Irish Stew 39
62. Korma Lamb Cutlets With Biryani Rice ... 40
63. Lamb And Grilled Vegetable Salad 41
64. Lamb And Strawberry Quinoa Tabouli 41
65. Lamb And Warm Artichoke Salad 42
66. Lamb Bake With Crispy Potato Topping . 42
67. Lamb Bake With Polenta 43
68. Lamb Chops In Ratatouille 43
69. Lamb Chops With Greek Fattoush Salad . 44
70. Lamb Chops With Greek Style Salad 44
71. Lamb Chops With An Italianate Stuffing. 45
72. Lamb Chops With Harissa Yoghurt 45
73. Lamb Chops With Lemony Asparagus Recipe 46
74. Lamb Chops With Oregano And Lemon. 47
75. Lamb Chops With Polenta 47
76. Lamb Chops With Polenta, Sun Dried Tomatoes And Pesto 48
77. Lamb Chops With Potato And Pea Salad. 48
78. Lamb Chops With Roast Vegetables 49
79. Lamb Chops With Roasted Ratatouille 49
80. Lamb Chops With Sundried Tomato And Basil Butter 50
81. Lamb Chops With White Bean Puree And Fresh Herb Salad 50
82. Lamb Cutlets And Rosemary Gravy 51
83. Lamb Cutlets With Bean Salad 51
84. Lamb Cutlets With Bean, Strawberry And Feta Salad 52
85. Lamb Cutlets With Braised Cannellini Beans Rosemary 52
86. Lamb Cutlets With Broad Bean Mash 53
87. Lamb Cutlets With Burghul And Eggplant Pilaf 53
88. Lamb Cutlets With Carrot And Broad Bean Salad Recipe 54
89. Lamb Cutlets With Char Grilled Vegetable Couscous 54
90. Lamb Cutlets With Chickpea Puree And Grilled Zucchini Salad 55
91. Lamb Cutlets With Chilli Olive Salsa 55
92. Lamb Cutlets With Eggplant Basil Fry Up And Quick Chilli Pickle 56
93. Lamb Cutlets With Feta And Prosciutto ... 57
94. Lamb Cutlets With Green Mash Mint Sauce 57
95. Lamb Cutlets With Haloumi 57
96. Lamb Cutlets With Lentil Salad 58
97. Lamb Cutlets With Lentil Salad And Mint And Watercress Pesto 59
98. Lamb Cutlets With Minted Potato Salad ... 59
99. Lamb Cutlets With Nam Jim And Coconut Rice 60
100. Lamb Cutlets With Orzo And Eggplant ... 60
101. Lamb Cutlets With Pistachio And Mint Pesto 61
102. Lamb Cutlets With Pistachio Pesto 61
103. Lamb Cutlets With Radish Salad Cinnamon Yoghurt 62
104. Lamb Cutlets With Risoni Salad 63
105. Lamb Cutlets With Roast Beetroot Salad Caraway Dressing 63
106. Lamb Cutlets With Spiced Carrot Salad 64
107. Lamb Cutlets With Spicy Parsnip Chips And Almond Sauce 64
108. Lamb Cutlets With Tomato Salsa 65
109. Lamb Cutlets With Warm Roasted Capsicum Salsa 66
110. Lamb Cutlets With Whipped Feta And Carrot Pickle 66
111. Lamb Cutlets With White Wine And Rosemary 67
112. Lamb Forequarter Chops With Chickpeas And Spinach 67
113. Lamb Loin Chops With Peppered Mash And Kale Salad 68
114. Lamb Neck Chops With Vegetables 68
115. Lamb Rack With Grilled Sweet Potato Salad And Olive Chimichurri 69
116. Lamb Tray Bake With Pesto, Tomatoes And Olives 70
117. Lamb Wellington Pops With Minted Pea Smash 70

118. Lamb With Green Bean Salad 71
119. Lamb With Grilled Cauliflower Steaks 71
120. Lamb With Kale Salad And Creamy Avocado Mint Sauce 71
121. Lamb With Lentil Salad 72
122. Lamb With Pumpkin And Lentil Winter Salad 72
123. Lamb With Roast Pumpkin Salad 73
124. Lamb With Warm Lentil Salad 74
125. Lemon And Herb Lamb Cutlets 74
126. Lemon And Oregano Lamb Chops 74
127. Lemon And Parsley Lamb Chops 75
128. Lemon And Thyme Lamb Chops 75
129. Lemon Chops With Greek Salad 76
130. Lemon Lamb Cutlets With Cucumber Salad 76
131. Lemon Lamb Cutlets With Spring Vegetables 77
132. Macadamia Crumbed Lamb Cutlets With Beetroot Dip 77
133. Magic Shake And Bake Crumbed Lamb Cutlets 78
134. Maple Glazed Lamb Sweet Potato Tray Bake 79
135. Marinated Lamb Chops 79
136. Marinated Lamb Chops With Potato And Corn Salad 80
137. Massaman Lamb Cutlets With Crunchy Coconut Potatoes 80
138. Meatlovers' Platter Recipe 81
139. Mediterranean Barbecued Lamb Chops 81
140. Minted Lamb Chops With Hot Potato Salad 82
141. Minted Lamb Cutlets 82
142. Minty Lamb Chops With Vegetable Crumble 83
143. Minty Lamb With Beetroot And Charred Broccoli 83
144. Mongolian Lamb Chops With Asian Greens 84
145. Mongolian Lamb Chops With Rice Salad . 84
146. Moroccan Lamb Chops With Quinoa Salad 85
147. Moroccan Lamb Cutlets With Cauliflower Pilaf 86
148. Moroccan Lamb Loin Chops With Mango Couscous 86

149. Moroccan Lamb With Bean Puree 87
150. Moroccan Lamb With Carrot And Radish Salad 87
151. Moroccan Spiced Lamb Chops With Moghrabieh And Roasted Beetroot 87
152. Moroccan Spiced Lamb Cutlets With Lentil Chickpea Salad 88
153. Moroccan Style Lamb Chops 89
154. Mustard Lamb Cutlets With Mint Aioli And Char Grilled Potatoes 89
155. Orange Chilli Lamb Cutlets With Warm White Bean Salad 90
156. Oregano And Lemon Lamb Chops With Greek Salad 91
157. Peppered Lamb Chops With Rhubarb And Fetta Couscous 91
158. Pesto Lamb Chops With Risoni Salad 92
159. Pita Cucumber Salad With Dukkah Lamb Cutlets 92
160. Portuguese Style BBQ Lamb Cutlets 93
161. Quick Garlic Lamb With Chargrilled Pineapple Slaw 93
162. Quick Harissa Lamb Chops With Asparagus And Bean Salad 94
163. Roast Lamb Racks With Mixed Herb Labne 94
164. Rosemary And Chilli Lamb Chops With Chargrilled Polenta 95
165. Rosemary And Garlic Lamb Chops 96
166. Rosemary Lamb Chops With Quinoa Salad 96
167. Rosemary Lamb Cutlets With Green Goddess Dressing 96
168. Rosemary, Lemon Seeded Mustard Lamb Cutlets 97
169. Scorched Tikka Chops With Tomato And Carrot Salad 98
170. Seared Lamb Forequarter Chops With Braised Spring Greens 98
171. Slow Cooker Lamb Chops In Red Wine Sauce 99
172. Slow Roasted Tomato Feta Salad With Grilled Lamb 99
173. Smoky Lamb Cutlets With Corn And Tomato Succotash 100
174. Spice Crusted Lamb Cutlets 101
175. Spiced BBQ Lamb Chops And Cos With

Coriander Lime Crema 101
176. Spiced Lamb Chops With Warm Chickpea Capsicum Salad 102
177. Spiced Lamb Cutlets With Chunky Veggie Salad 102
178. Spiced Lamb Cutlets With Garlic Tomato Salad 103
179. Spiced Lamb Cutlets With Mixed Lentil Salad 104
180. Spiced Lamb Cutlets With Peach Salad Recipe 105
181. Spicy Cajun Lamb Cutlets 105
182. Spicy Dukkah Crusted Lamb With Cauliflower Salad 106
183. Spicy Lamb Cutlets 106
184. Sticky Honey Lamb With Carrot And Lentil Slaw Recipe 106
185. Sticky Lamb Chops With Chickpea Salad 107
186. Sticky Lamb Cutlets With Tomato And Mint Salsa 107
187. Sticky Rosemary And Currant Glazed Lamb 108
188. Sumac Lamb Cutlets With Chickpeas And Pumpkin 108
189. Sumac Lamb With Cauliflower Fritters ... 109
190. Sumac Lamb With Tomato Bread Salad . 110
191. Sweet Lamb Chops With Coleslaw And Corn 110
192. T Rex Cutlets 111
193. Tandoori Cutlets With Beetroot Raita 111
194. Tandoori Lamb Cutlets With Cucumber Salad 112
195. Tandoori Lamb Cutlets With Cucumber Salad Recipe 112
196. Tandoori Lamb Salad 113
197. Teriyaki Lamb Cutlets 113
198. Teriyaki Lamb Cutlets With Stir Fried Greens 114
199. Thai Dressed Lamb Cutlets With Spring Salad 114
200. Yoghurt Marinated Lamb With Potato Mint Salad 115
201. Za'atar Lamb Cutlets With Carrot And Orange Salad 115
202. Za'atar Crusted Lamb Cutlets 116

INDEX 117
CONCLUSION 120

202 Awesome Lamb Chop And Cutlet Recipes

***

1. 17 Minute Spiced Lamb Cutlets With Couscous Salad Recipe

Serving: 0 | Prep: 0S | Ready in: 17mins

Ingredients

- 8 French-trimmed lamb cutlets
- 1 teaspoon ground cumin
- 2 tablespoons extra virgin olive oil
- 1 red onion, halved, thinly sliced
- 1 red capsicum, deseeded, thinly sliced
- 1 yellow capsicum, deseeded, thinly sliced
- 1 lemon, rind finely grated, halved
- 150g (3/4 cup) couscous
- 185ml (3/4 cup) boiling water
- 1 bunch fresh coriander, top leaves torn off
- 400g can chickpeas, rinsed, drained
- 90g (1/3 cup) Greek-style yoghurt
- 2 teaspoon harissa paste

Direction

- Sprinkle lamb with cumin. Season. Heat 1 1/2 tbsp. oil in a large non-stick frying pan over high heat. Add onion and capsicum. Season. Cook, stirring occasionally, for 5 minutes. Push capsicum mixture to the side. Add lamb. Cook, turning lamb and moving capsicum mixture, for 5 minutes or until lamb is cooked to your liking and capsicum mixture has softened. Remove from heat. Squeeze over 1 lemon half.
- Meanwhile, place couscous and lemon rind in a heatproof bowl. Add boiling water and remaining oil. Cover with a plate. Set aside for 5 minutes or until liquid is absorbed. Use a fork to separate grains. Add coriander, reserving a few sprigs, and chickpeas. Squeeze over remaining lemon half. Season. Stir to combine.
- Place yoghurt in a serving bowl. Swirl through harissa. Serve with lamb, capsicum mixture and couscous, topped with reserved coriander.

Nutrition Information

- Calories: 464.377 calories
- Total Fat: 18 grams fat
- Total Carbohydrate: 44.5 grams carbohydrates
- Saturated Fat: 4.5 grams saturated fat
- Protein: 26 grams protein

2. 5 Ingredient Dukkah Lamb Cutlets With Broccoli Rice

Serving: 4 | Prep: 15mins | Ready in: 35mins

Ingredients

- 200g vine-ripened cherry tomatoes
- 1 head broccoli, florets and stems coarsely chopped
- 12 Coles Australian Lamb Cutlets
- 2 tablespoons pistachio dukkah
- 200g tzatziki dip

Direction

- Preheat oven to 200°C. Line a baking tray with baking paper. Place tomatoes on tray. Season. Bake for 15-20 mins or until tomatoes begin to split.
- Meanwhile, place the broccoli in a food processor and process until finely chopped.

- Heat a large non-stick frying pan over high heat. Sprinkle both sides of lamb with half the dukkah.
- Cook for 2 mins each side for medium or until cooked to your liking. Transfer to a plate and cover with foil. Set aside for 5 mins to rest.
- While lamb is resting, add broccoli to the pan. Cook, tossing, for 3-5 mins or until bright green and cooked through.
- Serve the lamb and broccoli rice with the tomatoes, tzatziki and remaining dukkah.

Nutrition Information

- Calories: 325.279 calories
- Sugar: 3 grams sugar
- Protein: 27 grams protein
- Sodium: 232 milligrams sodium
- Saturated Fat: 8 grams saturated fat
- Total Carbohydrate: 4 grams carbohydrates
- Total Fat: 21 grams fat

3. Asian Style Lamb With Watermelon Coriander Salad

Serving: 4 | Prep: 25mins | Ready in: 35mins

Ingredients

- 1/3 cup (80ml) teriyaki marinade
- 2 garlic cloves, crushed
- 1/2 teaspoon Chinese five spice
- 8 Coles Australian Lamb Loin Chops
- 1 tablespoon soy sauce
- 2 teaspoons fish sauce
- 1 tablespoon white wine vinegar
- 1 teaspoon sesame oil
- 1 teaspoon brown sugar
- 60g pkt Coles Australian Baby Spinach
- 500g watermelon, peeled, cut into 3cm pieces
- 1 cup coriander leaves
- 2 spring onions, thinly sliced
- 1 long red chilli, sliced

Direction

- Combine the teriyaki marinade, garlic and Chinese five spice in a bowl. Add the lamb and turn to coat. Heat a barbecue grill or chargrill on medium-high. Cook the lamb for 4 mins each side for medium or until cooked to your liking. Transfer to a plate and cover with foil. Set aside for 5 mins to rest.
- Meanwhile, whisk the soy sauce, fish sauce, vinegar, oil and sugar in a small jug.
- Divide the spinach and watermelon among serving plates. Drizzle with the soy sauce mixture. Top with the lamb. Sprinkle with the coriander, onion and chilli to serve.

4. BBQ Lamb Cutlets With Tomato Ginger Curry Sauce

Serving: 4 | Prep: 15mins | Ready in: 30mins

Ingredients

- 2 large truss tomatoes (about 200g each), halved crossways
- 2 tablespoons olive oil, divided
- 10g ginger, peeled
- 1 garlic clove
- 1 lime
- 1 red birdseye chilli, very thinly sliced
- 2 teaspoons fish sauce
- 1 teaspoon caster sugar
- 1/2 teaspoon ground turmeric
- 12 lamb cutlets
- 2 zucchini (400g total), thinly sliced lengthways (about 4mm thick)
- 12 fresh coriander sprigs

Direction

- Prepare a barbecue for high heat.
- Using a small spoon, scoop out tomato seeds. Brush cut side of tomato halves with 2 teaspoons oil and barbecue cut side down for 5

mins, or until charred. Remove from barbecue to cool.
- Using fine holes of grater, grate cut side of tomato flesh into a bowl; discard tomato skins and tomato seeds that have not passed through grater. Grate ginger, garlic and lime zest into tomato flesh. Stir in 2 teaspoons lime juice, chilli, fish sauce, sugar and turmeric. Season with salt and more lime juice, if necessary.
- Toss zucchini with remaining oil and season with salt and pepper. Barbecue zucchini for about 1 1/2 mins per side, or until char marks form. Divide among 4 plates. Top each plate with 2 lamb cutlets and drizzle with tomato-curry sauce. Garnish with coriander and serve.

minutes over medium heat, then stir in vinegar, parsley and remaining oil.
- Season and serve with lamb cutlets.

Nutrition Information

- Calories: 595.588 calories
- Cholesterol: 112 milligrams cholesterol
- Sodium: 1079.46 milligrams sodium
- Saturated Fat: 12 grams saturated fat
- Total Carbohydrate: 16 grams carbohydrates
- Sugar: 5 grams sugar
- Protein: 39 grams protein
- Total Fat: 40 grams fat

5. Bacon Wrapped Lamb Cutlets With Beans And Fennel (gluten Free)

Serving: 4 | Prep: 25mins | Ready in: 40mins

Ingredients

- 8 frenched lamb cutlets
- 2 teaspoons English mustard
- 4 rashers of streaky bacon, halved widthways
- 1/4 cup (60ml) olive oil
- 800g canned cannellini beans, rinsed, drained
- 2 small fennel bulbs, thinly sliced
- 2 tablespoons white wine vinegar
- 1/4 cup fresh parsley leaves

Direction

- Spread cutlets with mustard and wrap meat in bacon. Secure with a toothpick.
- Heat 1 tablespoon oil in a large fry pan over high heat. Cook cutlets (in batches) for about 3 minutes each side until bacon is crisp and lamb is medium rare.
- Meanwhile, place beans and fennel in a pan with 2 tablespoons of water. Warm for 5

6. Baharat Lamb

Serving: 4 | Prep: 5mins | Ready in: 15mins

Ingredients

- 2 tablespoons olive oil
- 12 lamb cutlets, trimmed
- tabouli, tzatziki, Lebanese bread, to serve
- 1 1/2 tablespoons sweet paprika
- 1 tablespoon ground black pepper
- 3 teaspoons McCormick Ground Cumin
- 2 teaspoons ground coriander
- 2 teaspoons ground cinnamon
- 2 teaspoons ground cloves
- 1 teaspoon ground cardamom
- 1/2 teaspoon ground star anise
- pinch of ground nutmeg

Direction

- Make baharat spice rub: Place ingredients in a bowl. Mix well to combine.
- Combine oil and 2 tablespoons spice rub in a bowl. Brush over both sides lamb cutlets. Cover and refrigerate for 30 minutes, if time permits.
- Preheat a barbecue plate on medium heat until hot. Cook lamb for 3 minutes each side for

medium or until cooked to your liking. Serve with tabouli, tzatziki and Lebanese bread.

7. Baked Five Spice Lamb Cutlets

Serving: 4 | Prep: 10mins | Ready in: 40mins

Ingredients

- 1/2 cup dried multigrain breadcrumbs
- 1 tablespoon MasterFoods® Sesame Seeds
- 2 teaspoons Chinese five spice powder
- 1 tablespoon finely chopped fresh chives
- 1 egg
- 12 lamb cutlets, trimmed
- canola oil cooking spray
- crunchy Asian salad, to serve

Direction

- Preheat oven to 180°C/160°C fan-forced. Line a baking tray with baking paper. Combine breadcrumbs, sesame seeds, five spice and chives in a large, shallow bowl. Season with salt and pepper.
- Whisk egg in a bowl. Dip lamb in egg, then breadcrumb mixture. Place on prepared tray. Spray cutlets lightly with oil. Bake for 30 minutes or until browned and cooked through, turning halfway during cooking. Serve with salad.

Nutrition Information

- Calories: 375.947 calories
- Total Carbohydrate: 11 grams carbohydrates
- Protein: 39 grams protein
- Cholesterol: 175 milligrams cholesterol
- Sodium: 239.08 milligrams sodium
- Total Fat: 19 grams fat
- Saturated Fat: 7 grams saturated fat
- Sugar: 1 grams sugar

8. Baked Lamb Chops With Fetta Crumble

Serving: 4 | Prep: 20mins | Ready in: 75mins

Ingredients

- 800g cream delight potatoes, unpeeled, roughly chopped
- 1 lemon, halved, thinly sliced
- 1/4 cup lemon juice
- 1 teaspoon dried oregano
- 1/4 cup Cobram Estate classic flavour extra virgin olive oil
- 8 lamb loin chops
- 100g Greek fetta, crumbled
- 1 tablespoon lemon zest (see note)
- 1/4 cup chopped fresh flat-leaf parsley leaves
- 200g steamed green beans, to serve

Direction

- Preheat oven to 200C/180C fan-forced. Place potatoes, lemon, lemon juice, oregano and 2 tablespoons oil in a large bowl. Toss to combine. Place in a 5.5cmdeep, 23cm x 34cm oval roasting pan. Season with salt and pepper. Bake for 45 minutes or until golden and tender.
- Meanwhile, heat remaining oil in a large frying pan over medium-high heat. Cook lamb for 2 minutes each side or until browned.
- Place lamb on potatoes. Sprinkle with feta. Bake for a further 7 to 8 minutes for medium or until lamb is cooked to your liking. Top with lemon zest and parsley. Serve with steamed green beans.

Nutrition Information

- Calories: 579.336 calories
- Cholesterol: 103 milligrams cholesterol
- Total Carbohydrate: 24.1 grams carbohydrates
- Sodium: 421 milligrams sodium
- Total Fat: 33.4 grams fat

- Saturated Fat: 11.4 grams saturated fat
- Sodium: 101.88 milligrams sodium

9. Baked Lamb Chops With Pumpkin

Serving: 4 | Prep: 10mins | Ready in: 60mins

Ingredients

- 1 (680g) golden nugget pumpkin, cut into wedges, deseeded
- Olive oil cooking spray
- 8 lamb loin chops, trimmed
- 1 cup orange marmalade
- 1/4 cup orange juice
- 2cm piece ginger, peeled, finely grated
- 175g baby green beans, trimmed, steamed

Direction

- Preheat oven to 200°C. Line a baking tray with baking paper. Place pumpkin wedges onto prepared tray. Spray with oil. Season with salt and pepper. Bake for 15 minutes.
- Meanwhile, place chops into a large ovenproof baking dish. Combine marmalade, orange juice and ginger in a bowl. Season with salt and pepper. Spoon mixture onto chops. Turn to coat. Place chops into oven under pumpkin. Bake both for a further 35 minutes or until chops are cooked through and pumpkin is golden and tender. Place chops onto serving plates. Drizzle with pan juices. Serve with pumpkin and beans.

Nutrition Information

- Calories: 630.96 calories
- Protein: 32 grams protein
- Cholesterol: 84 milligrams cholesterol
- Total Carbohydrate: 70 grams carbohydrates
- Total Fat: 23 grams fat
- Saturated Fat: 10 grams saturated fat
- Sugar: 67 grams sugar

10. Balinese Lamb Chops

Serving: 4 | Prep: 5mins | Ready in: 45mins

Ingredients

- Olive oil cooking spray
- 1 brown onion, finely chopped
- 2 tablespoons crunchy peanut butter
- 1 tablespoon sweet chilli sauce
- 1 tablespoon ketcap manis
- 270ml can light coconut milk
- 8 lamb chump chops, trimmed
- 2 x 350g packets egg noodles, cooked
- 2 bunches baby bok choy, steamed

Direction

- Preheat oven to 200°C. Heat a non-stick frying pan over medium heat. Spray with oil. Add onion. Cook, stirring, for 3 minutes or until soft. Add peanut butter, sweet chilli, kecap manis and coconut milk to frying pan. Stir until well combined. Bring to the boil.
- Arrange chops in a single layer in an oven-proof casserole dish. Pour over sauce. Turn to coat. Bake, uncovered, for 35 minutes or until cooked through. Serve with noodles and baby bok choy.

Nutrition Information

- Calories: 684.974 calories
- Total Carbohydrate: 56 grams carbohydrates
- Saturated Fat: 14 grams saturated fat
- Sugar: 7 grams sugar
- Protein: 44 grams protein
- Sodium: 627.32 milligrams sodium
- Total Fat: 30 grams fat

11. Barbecued Moroccan Lamb With Potatoes

Serving: 4 | Prep: 15mins | Ready in: 45mins

Ingredients

- 4 small (about 200g each) brushed (sebago) potatoes, peeled
- 5 teaspoons ground coriander
- 3 teaspoons ground cumin
- 2 teaspoons sweet paprika
- 1 teaspoon ground ginger
- 1 teaspoon dried garlic flakes
- 1/4 teaspoon ground cardamom
- 1/4 teaspoon cayenne pepper
- 12 (about 900g) lamb cutlets, excess fat trimmed
- 2 tablespoons olive oil
- 2 tablespoons fresh lemon juice
- Dressed baby spinach leaves, to serve

Direction

- Place the potatoes in a medium saucepan and cover with cold water. Bring to the boil over high heat. Reduce heat to medium-high and cook, uncovered, for 8 minutes or until just tender. Drain and set aside to cool for 5 minutes. Cut potatoes into 1cm-thick rounds. Preheat oven to 160i¿½C.
- Meanwhile, combine the coriander, cumin, paprika, ginger, garlic, cardamom and cayenne pepper in a small bowl. Place the lamb cutlets in a large, shallow non-aluminium dish. Sprinkle the spice blend over both sides of the lamb cutlets and use your fingertips to rub into the lamb.
- Preheat a barbecue plate or heavy-based frying pan on high. Add the oil and heat for 30 seconds or until hot. Add the potato slices and cook for 4-5 minutes each side or until golden and tender. Transfer the potatoes to an ovenproof dish and place in preheated oven to keep warm.
- Add the lamb cutlets to the hot barbecue plate or frying pan. Drizzle with lemon juice (this prevents the spices from burning) and cook for 3 minutes each side for medium or until cooked to your liking.
- Serve the lamb cutlets with the potatoes and dressed spinach leaves.

Nutrition Information

- Calories: 581.248 calories
- Sodium: 152.31 milligrams sodium
- Total Fat: 30 grams fat
- Total Carbohydrate: 27 grams carbohydrates
- Protein: 48 grams protein

12. Barbecued Lamb Chops With Romesco Sauce

Serving: 0 | Prep: 15mins | Ready in: 45mins

Ingredients

- 2 red capsicums (400g total)
- 1 red truss tomato (140g)
- 5 x 2cm slices Coles Bakery French Stick* (60g total)
- 5 tablespoons olive oil, divided
- 30g toasted slivered almonds
- 1 tablespoon red wine vinegar
- 1 garlic clove
- 8 lamb loin chops (about 120g each)
- 2 tablespoons fresh oregano leaves

Direction

- Prepare a barbecue for medium-high heat. In a large bowl, toss the capsicums, tomato and French stick with 1 tbsp. of the oil. Barbecue the vegetables and bread, turning as needed, for about 3 mins for the bread, or until it is toasted with char marks. Transfer the bread to a chopping board. Continue barbecuing the capsicums and tomato, turning as needed, until they are charred all over and soft, about 12 mins for the tomato and 20 mins for the

capsicums. Transfer the vegetables to the chopping board to cool slightly.
- Remove the stem and seeds from the capsicums and transfer the capsicum flesh to a blender. Coarsely chop the tomato and bread and transfer to the blender. Add almonds, vinegar, garlic and 2 tbsp. of the oil. Season with sea salt flakes. Blend until pureed, but not completely smooth. Season to taste with more salt or vinegar, if necessary.
- Coat the lamb chops with 2 tsp. of oil and season with salt and pepper. Barbecue, turning once, for about 3 mins each side, or until char marks form and an instant-read thermometer inserted into the center of the chops registers 54C. Transfer to a platter and spoon over the remaining 1 1/2 tablespoon of oil. Set aside to rest for 5 mins.
- Sprinkle oregano over the lamb chops and serve with the romesco sauce.

13. Barbecued Lamb Cutlets With Fresh Mint Red Wine Vinegar Sauce

Serving: 4 | Prep: 40mins | Ready in: 50mins

Ingredients

- 1 cup (not packed) fresh mint leaves
- 1/2 cup good-quality red wine vinegar
- 2 tablespoons caster sugar
- 1 teaspoon sea salt flakes, plus more for seasoning
- 4 garlic cloves, finely chopped
- 2 tablespoons finely grated lemon zest
- 2 tablespoons olive oil
- 1 tablespoon chopped fresh rosemary
- 12 lamb cutlets (about 80g each)

Direction

- Place the mint in a medium bowl. In a small saucepan, bring the vinegar, sugar, and 1/2 cup of water to a boil over medium-high heat, stirring until the sugar dissolves. Pour the vinegar mixture over the mint and steep for about 30 minutes. Mix in 1 teaspoon of salt and strain the sauce.
- Meanwhile, prepare a barbecue for medium-high heat. In a large bowl, mix the garlic, lemon, oil, and rosemary. Coat the lamb cutlets with the garlic mixture. Marinate at room temperature while the vinegar-mint sauce steeps.
- Season the lamb generously with salt and pepper. Barbecue the lamb for about 2 minutes per side, or until nicely charred on the outside and the internal temperature of the cutlets is 50°C for medium-rare doneness. Set aside to rest for 3 minutes.
- Serve the lamb with the vinegar-mint sauce.

14. Barbecued Lamb Cutlets With Two Salsas

Serving: 8 | Prep: 145mins | Ready in: 190mins

Ingredients

- 24 lamb cutlets, trimmed
- 2 tablespoons extra virgin olive oil
- 2 tablespoons roughly chopped fresh oregano
- 2 tablespoons extra virgin olive oil
- 1 red onion, finely chopped
- 1 medium eggplant, finely chopped
- 1 large red capsicum, finely chopped
- 1 garlic clove, crushed
- 400g can diced tomatoes
- 2 teaspoons red wine vinegar
- 2 tablespoons chopped fresh basil leaves
- 230g jar pitted green Sicilian olives, drained, roughly chopped
- 1 tablespoon drained capers, roughly chopped
- 1 garlic clove, crushed
- 2 tablespoons lemon juice
- 2 tablespoons extra virgin olive oil
- 1/4 cup roughly chopped fresh flat-leaf parsley

Direction

- Place lamb in a large, shallow glass or ceramic dish. Combine oil and oregano in a bowl. Spoon over lamb. Turn to coat. Season with pepper. Cover. Refrigerate for 2 hours.
- To make Eggplant and Tomato Salsa, heat oil in a large frying pan over medium heat. Cook onion, eggplant and capsicum, stirring occasionally, for 5 minutes or until onion starts to soften. Reduce heat to low. Cover. Cook, stirring occasionally, for 15 to 20 minutes or until eggplant is very tender. Add garlic and tomatoes. Season with salt and pepper. Cook, uncovered, for 10 minutes or until mixture has thickened. Remove from heat. Stir in vinegar and basil.
- Heat a barbecue chargrill or chargrill pan on medium-high heat. Cook lamb, in batches, for 3 to 4 minutes each side for medium, or until browned and cooked to your liking. Transfer to a plate. Cover loosely with foil. Stand for 5 minutes to rest.
- Meanwhile, make Green Olive and Caper Salsa: combine olives, capers, garlic, lemon juice, oil and parsley in a bowl. Season well with pepper.
- Serve cutlets with eggplant salsa and olive salsa.

Nutrition Information

- Calories: 396.74 calories
- Total Fat: 27.6 grams fat
- Saturated Fat: 7.4 grams saturated fat
- Protein: 29.9 grams protein
- Cholesterol: 88 milligrams cholesterol
- Sodium: 395 milligrams sodium
- Total Carbohydrate: 6.5 grams carbohydrates

15. Barbecued Mint Lamb Chops With Charred Corn And Chilli Slaw

Serving: 4 | Prep: 10mins | Ready in: 25mins

Ingredients

- 4 (160g each) Coles Australian lamb forequarter chops
- 1/3 cup (80ml) mint jelly, warmed
- 4 corn cobs, husks removed, halved
- 250g pkt Coles Brand coleslaw mix
- 1 celery stick, thinly sliced
- 1 long red chilli, cut into thin strips
- 1/4 cup (60ml) Coles Brand coleslaw dressing
- Mint leaves, to serve

Direction

- Heat a barbecue grill or chargrill on medium-high. Cook lamb, basting with mint jelly, for 4 mins each side or until cooked to your liking. Rest, covered with foil, for 5 minutes. Season.
- Cook corn cobs on grill, turning, for 7 mins or until charred.
- Meanwhile, combine coleslaw, celery, chili and dressing in a large bowl.
- Serve lamb with corn and coleslaw, and top with mint.

16. Barbecued Spiced Lamb Chops With Pumpkin Salad

Serving: 4 | Prep: 20mins | Ready in: 40mins

Ingredients

- 1 large lemon
- 3 cloves garlic
- 1 teaspoon dried chilli flakes
- 2 teaspoons fennel seeds
- 1 tablespoon rosemary leaves
- 90ml extra virgin olive oil
- 8 lamb loin chops

- 1/4 (800g) jap pumpkin
- 1 bunch rocket
- 100g goat's cheese

Direction

- Preheat a barbecue or chargrill pan over medium-high heat. Meanwhile, zest and juice the lemon, keeping the zest and juice separate. Using a mortar and pestle, grind garlic and 1 teaspoon salt to a paste, then stir in lemon zest, 2 tablespoons lemon juice, chilli flakes, fennel seeds, rosemary and 80ml (1/3 cup) oil. Reserve remaining juice. Transfer one-third of the marinade to a small bowl and reserve for serving.
- Divide remaining marinade between 2 large bowls. Add lamb to 1 bowl, toss well to coat, then marinate for 5 minutes.
- Meanwhile, cut pumpkin into 2cm-thick wedges, then halve wedges widthwise. Place in a single layer on a large, microwave-safe plate. Cover with plastic wrap and microwave on full power for 5 minutes or until almost tender. Drain liquid, then add pumpkin to second large bowl with marinade. Toss to coat.
- Barbecue lamb for 4 minutes each side or until almost cooked through. Rest for 5 minutes. Meanwhile, barbecue pumpkin for 2 minutes each side or until lightly charred.
- To make salad, whisk 1 teaspoon reserved lemon juice, remaining 2 teaspoons oil and a pinch of salt in a large bowl. Add rocket and toss to combine. Crumble over goat's cheese.
- Divide lamb and pumpkin among plates and drizzle with reserved marinade. Serve with salad.

Nutrition Information

- Calories: 657.489 calories
- Total Fat: 49 grams fat
- Saturated Fat: 17 grams saturated fat
- Total Carbohydrate: 15 grams carbohydrates
- Sugar: 13 grams sugar
- Protein: 37 grams protein
- Cholesterol: 96 milligrams cholesterol
- Sodium: 166.32 milligrams sodium

17. Barbecued Tandoori Lamb Cutlets With Coconut Rice Recipe

Serving: 4 | Prep: 0S | Ready in: 10mins

Ingredients

- 2 tbs gluten-free tandoori paste
- 1 tbs olive oil
- 8 French-trimmed lamb cutlets
- 200g green beans
- 2 x 250g pkt Tilda Microwave Coconut Steamed Basmati Rice
- 50g (1/2 cup) natural sliced almonds
- 80g (1/2 cup) currants
- 100g baby spinach
- Tzatziki dip, to serve

Direction

- Put the kettle on. Preheat a barbecue grill or chargrill pan on medium-high.
- While the kettle boils and grill heats up, combine tandoori paste and oil in a large bowl. Add lamb and toss well to coat. Trim or shred beans and place in a heatproof bowl.
- Pour the boiling water over the beans and set aside to blanch. Grill the lamb for 2-3 minutes each side for medium or until cooked to your liking.
- Meanwhile, microwave the rice following packet directions. Transfer to a large bowl. Add the almonds and currants. Toss until well combined.
- Drain beans. Divide rice mixture, beans and spinach among serving plates. Top with lamb. Season and serve with a dollop of tzatziki.

Nutrition Information

- Calories: 542.291 calories

- Total Fat: 26.3 grams fat
- Protein: 23.8 grams protein
- Saturated Fat: 8.2 grams saturated fat
- Total Carbohydrate: 49.9 grams carbohydrates

18. Basil And Goat's Cheese Lamb Racks

Serving: 4 | Prep: 30mins | Ready in: 60mins

Ingredients

- 1 1/2 cups fresh breadcrumbs (made from day-old bread)
- 1/4 cup basil leaves
- 2 tablespoons Coles Brand Pure Olive Oil
- 180g goat's fetta, crumbled
- 1/4 cup semi-dried tomatoes, from the deli, coarsely chopped
- 2 Coles Australian Lamb Racks (8 cutlets on each)
- 2 zucchini, thickly sliced diagonally
- 400g Perino tomatoes
- 1/2 cup kalamata olives, from the deli
- Baby rocket leaves, to serve

Direction

- Preheat oven to 200C or 180C fan forced. Process the breadcrumbs, 2 tablespoons basil and half the oil to combine.
- Finely chop remaining basil. Combine basil, feta and semi-dried tomatoes in a medium bowl. Use a sharp knife to cut along the length of each lamb rack, close to the bone, about 3cm deep, to create a pocket. Divide the feta mixture evenly among the pockets. Use kitchen string to tie around each rack to secure. Place in a roasting pan. Press the breadcrumb mixture firmly onto the lamb racks. Arrange zucchini around the lamb racks. Drizzle with remaining oil. Season.
- Roast for 20 minutes. Arrange the tomato and olives over zucchini mixture. Roast for a further 10 mins for medium or until cooked to your liking. Set aside, covered, for 10 mins to rest.
- Carve the lamb racks into portions. Arrange the vegetable mixture, rocket and lamb on platters.

19. Best Ever Grilled Lamb Chops With Lemon Myrtle Butter

Serving: 4 | Prep: 10mins | Ready in: 30mins

Ingredients

- 600g baby chat potatoes
- 2 large carrots, peeled, sliced diagonally
- 1 cup frozen peas
- 80g butter, softened
- 2 teaspoons dried lemon myrtle
- 2 teaspoons dijon mustard
- 8 (150g each) lamb loin chops
- 1 tablespoon olive oil

Direction

- Place potatoes in a saucepan. Cover with cold water. Bring to the boil over high heat. Reduce heat to medium. Cook for 12 minutes, adding carrot for the last 4 minutes of cooking time and peas for the last 1 minute of cooking time. Drain. Return to pan. Cover to keep warm.
- Combine butter, lemon myrtle and mustard together in a small bowl. Season with salt and pepper. Add half the butter mixture to vegetables in pan. Toss carefully to coat. Cover to keep warm. Season with salt and pepper.
- Meanwhile, preheat grill to high. Place chops on a wire rack set over a large baking tray. Brush chops on both sides with oil. Season with salt and pepper. Place chops under grill, 5cm away from heat. Grill for 4 minutes. Turn. Grill for a further 4 minutes for medium or until cooked to your liking. Cover loosely with foil. Set aside for 5 minutes to rest.
- Serve chops with vegetables and remaining lemon myrtle butter.

Nutrition Information

- Calories: 595.11 calories
- Cholesterol: 131 milligrams cholesterol
- Total Fat: 34.6 grams fat
- Total Carbohydrate: 27.6 grams carbohydrates
- Protein: 38.9 grams protein
- Sodium: 505 milligrams sodium
- Saturated Fat: 17.7 grams saturated fat

20. Black Bean Lamb Cutlets With Roasted Spring Veggies

Serving: 4 | Prep: 10mins | Ready in: 30mins

Ingredients

- 1/3 cup (80ml) black bean sauce
- 2 teaspoons finely grated ginger
- 1 garlic clove, crushed
- 1 tablespoon honey
- 2 tablespoons sweet chilli sauce
- 12 Coles Australian Lamb Cutlets
- 1 tablespoon olive oil
- 1 bunch asparagus, woody ends trimmed
- 8 spring onions, cut into 10cm lengths
- 1 bunch baby pak choy, washed, halved
- Coriander leaves, to serve
- Thinly sliced long red chilli, to serve

Direction

- Preheat oven to 180C. Combine the black bean sauce, ginger, garlic, honey and sweet chili sauce in a large shallow glass or ceramic dish. Add the lamb and turn to coat. Season.
- Heat a barbecue grill or chargrill on high. Remove the lamb from the black bean sauce mixture, reserving the mixture. Cook the lamb on the grill for 1 min each side or until just brown.
- Arrange the asparagus, spring onion and pak choy in a large baking dish. Drizzle with oil. Season. Top with lamb and bake for 12-15 mins or until the lamb is cooked to your liking and the vegetables are tender.
- Meanwhile, place the reserved black bean mixture and 2 tablespoons water in a small saucepan over medium-high heat. Bring to the boil. Reduce heat to medium-low and bring to a simmer. Cook for 2 mins or until slightly thickened.
- Sprinkle the lamb and vegetables with coriander and chili. Drizzle with the black bean dressing to serve.

21. Braised Tomato Lamb Chops With Fetta

Serving: 4 | Prep: 20mins | Ready in: 140mins

Ingredients

- 4 Coles Australian lamb forequarter chops
- 400g can crushed tomato
- 1 cup (250ml) chicken stock
- 2 bay leaves
- 2 brown onions, chopped
- 2 garlic cloves, sliced
- 1/2 teaspoon ground allspice
- 2 zucchini, sliced
- 1 red capsicum, coarsely chopped
- 200g green beans, halved
- 60g fetta, crumbled
- 1/4 cup flat-leaf parsley leaves
- Coles Bakery Pane di Casa bread, to serve

Direction

- Preheat oven to 170C. Place the lamb, tomato, stock, bay leaves, onion, garlic and allspice in a large baking dish. Season. Cover and bake for 1 hour.
- Uncover and stir in zucchini and capsicum. Bake for 45 mins or until tender. Add the green beans. Bake for a further 15 mins or until beans are tender. Sprinkle with feta and parsley. Serve with bread.

22. Cajun Lamb With American Slaw And Corn

Serving: 4 | Prep: 15mins | Ready in: 25mins

Ingredients

- 4 cobs corn, husks and silks removed
- 2 tablespoons olive oil
- 1 tablespoon Cajun seasoning
- 12 Coles Australian Lamb Cutlets
- 400g Coles American Coleslaw Kit
- 1/3 cup (25g) finely grated parmesan
- 1 teaspoon smoked paprika
- 20g butter, chopped

Direction

- Preheat a barbecue grill or chargrill on high. Cook the corn, turning, for 10 mins or until charred and tender.
- Combine oil and Cajun seasoning in a shallow glass or ceramic dish. Add lamb and toss to coat. Cook lamb on the grill for 3 mins each side or until cooked to your liking. Transfer to a plate. Cover with foil and set aside for 5 mins to rest.
- Meanwhile, prepare coleslaw following packet directions.
- Combine the parmesan and paprika in a bowl. Spread the corn with butter and sprinkle with parmesan mixture. Season.
- Divide lamb, corn and coleslaw among serving plates.

23. Char Grilled Lamb Chops With Greek Salad

Serving: 4 | Prep: 10mins | Ready in: 20mins

Ingredients

- 3 small field tomatoes, cut into wedges
- 1 continental cucumber, peeled, halved lengthwise, seeded and sliced across
- 1/4 small red onion, very thinly sliced
- 1 tablespoon Coles red wine vinegar
- 1/4 cup Coles extra-virgin olive oil
- 100g Coles Australian-style feta
- 2 teaspoons dried oregano
- 2 teaspoons paprika
- 4 Coles Butcher lamb forequarter chops
- 2 cloves garlic, finely chopped
- 1 tablespoon Coles olive oil

Direction

- Prepare a barbecue to medium-high heat.
- To marinade the lamb: Sprinkle the oregano, paprika, and garlic over the lamb. Drizzle 1 tablespoon of olive oil over the lamb and marinate for 10 minutes at room temperature.
- Season lamb with salt and pepper on both sides, drizzle 1 tablespoon of oil over the lamb then place on the hot char grill barbecue and cook for 3-4 minutes on each side or until just pale pink in the centre.
- Remove from the char grill and rest for 3-4 minutes.
- Meanwhile, prepare the Greek salad: In a large mixing bowl, combine the tomatoes, cucumbers and onion.
- In a separate mixing bowl, whisk the vinegar and slowly drizzle in the olive oil, season to taste with salt and pepper.
- Toss the salad with enough of the vinaigrette to coat and season to taste with salt and pepper.
- Divide the salad among 4 serving plates. Top each salad with a grilled lamb chop and crumble the feta cheese over the salads.
- Drizzle some of the remaining vinaigrette over the lamb and salad and serve.

Nutrition Information

- Calories: 706.962 calories
- Saturated Fat: 12.7 grams saturated fat

- Total Carbohydrate: 9.4 grams carbohydrates
- Sugar: 3.8 grams sugar
- Cholesterol: 247 milligrams cholesterol
- Total Fat: 40.3 grams fat
- Protein: 75.4 grams protein
- Sodium: 476 milligrams sodium

24. Chargrilled Garlic And Pepper Lamb Chops With Mixed Bean Salad

Serving: 4 | Prep: 15mins | Ready in: 25mins

Ingredients

- 2 tablespoons extra virgin olive oil
- 2 teaspoons cracked black pepper
- 4 garlic cloves, crushed
- 8 Coles Australian Lamb Loin Chops
- 100g snow peas, trimmed, sliced lengthways
- 100g green beans, trimmed
- 400g can four-bean mix, drained, rinsed
- 60g Coles Brand Australian Baby Spinach
- 250g punnet cherry tomatoes, halved
- 1 tablespoon red wine vinegar
- Flat-leaf parsley leaves, to serve

Direction

- Combine 1 tablespoon of the oil with the pepper and garlic in a large bowl. Season with salt. Add lamb and turn to coat.
- Heat a barbecue grill, chargrill or frying pan on medium-high. Cook lamb for 3-4 mins each side or until cooked to your liking. Transfer to a plate and cover with foil. Set aside for 5 mins to rest.
- Meanwhile, cook snow peas and green beans in a medium saucepan of salted boiling water for 2 mins or until just tender. Rinse under cold water. Drain.
- Combine snow peas and green beans in a large bowl with four-bean mix, spinach, tomato, vinegar and remaining oil. Season.
- Sprinkle lamb with parsley. Serve with salad.

25. Chargrilled Lemon And Rosemary Lamb Cutlets Recipe

Serving: 4 | Prep: 10mins | Ready in: 25mins

Ingredients

- 1 cup (250ml) buttermilk
- 1 tbs finely grated lemon rind
- 2 tbs chopped rosemary leaves
- 1 long green chilli, seeded, finely chopped (optional)
- 1 garlic clove, crushed
- 12 Coles Australian Lamb Cutlets
- 6 tomatoes, cut into wedges
- 1 cup mint leaves
- 60g pkt Coles Australian Baby Rocket
- 1 lemon, juiced
- 1 1/2 tbs olive oil

Direction

- Combine buttermilk, lemon rind, rosemary, chilli, if using, and garlic in a large bowl. Season. Add lamb and turn to coat. Set aside for 15 mins to develop the flavours.
- Place the tomato, mint and rocket in a large bowl. Drizzle with the lemon juice and oil. Season and gently toss to combine.
- Heat a barbecue grill or chargrill on medium. Drain lamb from the buttermilk mixture. Cook for 2 1/2 mins each side for medium or until cooked to your liking. Set aside for 5 mins to rest. Serve the lamb with the salad.

26. Charred Lamb Chops With Greek Salad

Serving: 4 | Prep: 20mins | Ready in: 25mins

Ingredients

- 8 Coles Australian Lamb Loin Chops, excess fat trimmed
- 2 teaspoons ground paprika
- 3 teaspoons dried oregano
- 2 tablespoons olive oil
- 1 red capsicum, seeded, coarsely chopped
- 1 Lebanese cucumber, halved lengthways, thinly sliced
- 200g Perino tomatoes, halved
- 1 red onion, thinly sliced
- 1 tablespoons red wine vinegar
- 100g reduced-fat fetta, crumbled
- 1/2 cup (75g) pitted kalamata olives

Direction

- Combine the lamb, paprika, 2 teaspoons of the oregano and half the oil in a large bowl. Season and toss to combine.
- Heat a chargrill on medium-high. Cook the lamb for 2 mins each side for medium or until cooked to your liking. Transfer to a plate. Cover with foil and set aside for 5 mins to rest.
- Meanwhile, combine the capsicum, cucumber, tomato and onion in a large bowl. Drizzle with vinegar and remaining oil. Season. Sprinkle with feta, olives and remaining oregano. Serve immediately with the lamb.

Nutrition Information

- Calories: 405.583 calories
- Sodium: 480 milligrams sodium
- Saturated Fat: 7 grams saturated fat
- Protein: 37 grams protein
- Sugar: 7 grams sugar
- Total Fat: 24 grams fat
- Total Carbohydrate: 8 grams carbohydrates

27. Cheesy Cutlets With Avocado Dip

Serving: 4 | Prep: 45mins | Ready in: 60mins

Ingredients

- 1/2 cup plain flour
- 2 eggs, lightly beaten
- 1 cup dried breadcrumbs
- 40g tasty cheese, grated
- 8 lamb cutlets
- 1 large avocado
- 1 tablespoon sour cream
- 1/2 small lemon, juiced
- 1 green onion, thinly sliced
- vegetable oil, for cooking

Direction

- Place flour and eggs in separate shallow dishes. Combine breadcrumbs and cheese on a large, flat plate. Dip cutlets, 1 at a time, into flour to coat, shaking off excess. Dip into egg, then into breadcrumb mixture, pressing on with fingertips to secure. Place on a plate. Cover and refrigerate for 30 minutes (this helps keep crumbs on when cooking).
- Cut avocado in half. Remove stone. Scoop out flesh onto a clean board. Mash with a fork until almost smooth. Transfer to a bowl. Add sour cream, 1 tablespoon lemon juice and onion. Stir to combine.
- Meanwhile preheat oven to 180°C. Pour oil into a large frying pan until 5mm deep. Heat over medium heat. Cook cutlets, in batches, for 2 minutes each side or until light golden. Transfer to a baking tray. Place in oven. Cook for 5 minutes for medium or until cooked to your liking. Serve cutlets with avocado dip.

28. Chermoula Lamb Cutlets With Coconut Pilaf

Serving: 4 | Prep: 15mins | Ready in: 35mins

Ingredients

- 1/3 cup olive oil
- 1 brown onion, halved, sliced
- 1/3 cup shredded coconut
- 1/3 cup flaked almonds
- 1/4 cup currants
- 3 1/2 tablespoons chermoula spice rub (we used Zest brand)
- 2 cups jasmine rice
- 12 (70g each) lamb cutlets
- lemon wedges, to serve

Direction

- Heat 2 tablespoons of olive oil in a large, heavy-based saucepan over medium heat. Add onion. Cook for 2 to 3 minutes or until onion is tender. Add coconut, almonds, currants and 1 teaspoon of chermoula rub. Cook, stirring, for 1 to 2 minutes or until coconut just turns golden.
- Add rice. Stir to combine. Add 3 cups of cold water. Bring to the boil. Cover and reduce heat to low. Simmer for 10 minutes or until water is absorbed. Remove from heat. Set aside for 12 minutes or until rice is tender.
- Meanwhile, rub cutlets with remaining chermoula. Season with salt and pepper. Heat remaining oil in a large non-stick frying pan over medium-high heat. Cook cutlets, in batches, for 3 minutes each side for medium or until cooked to your liking. Remove to a plate. Serve cutlets with pilaf and lemon wedges.

Nutrition Information

- Calories: 999.259 calories
- Total Fat: 48 grams fat
- Protein: 50 grams protein
- Sodium: 187.43 milligrams sodium
- Cholesterol: 141 milligrams cholesterol
- Saturated Fat: 14 grams saturated fat
- Total Carbohydrate: 89 grams carbohydrates
- Sugar: 8 grams sugar

29. Chermoula Lamb Cutlets With Dried Fruit Couscous

Serving: 4 | Prep: 20mins | Ready in: 30mins

Ingredients

- 200g dried fruit medley
- Zest and juice of 1 lemon, plus wedges to serve
- 1 teaspoon ground cumin
- 1 teaspoon ground coriander
- 2 teaspoons sweet paprika
- 1/4 cup (60ml) olive oil
- 1/3 cup finely chopped flat-leaf parsley leaves, plus extra to garnish
- 1/3 cup finely chopped coriander leaves
- 12 French-trimmed lamb cutlets
- 1 1/4 cups (250g) couscous
- Thick Greek yoghurt, to serve

Direction

- In a bowl, stir the dried fruit with 1/4 cup (60ml) boiling water. Set aside for 10 minutes to plump.
- Place lemon zest and juice, spices, olive oil, half the parsley and half the coriander in a food processor, and process until combined. Coat cutlets in marinade, then set aside.
- Prepare the couscous according to packet instructions. Drain the dried fruit and toss through the couscous with the remaining herbs. Season with sea salt and freshly ground black pepper.
- Heat a chargrill pan, barbecue or fry pan on high heat. Cook cutlets for
- 1-2 minutes each side or until cooked as desired. Sprinkle cutlets with extra parsley and serve with the couscous, lemon wedges and thick Greek yoghurt.

30. Chilli And Orange Lamb Chops With Pearl Couscous Salad

Serving: 4 | Prep: 30mins | Ready in: 60mins

Ingredients

- 700g pumpkin, peeled, cut into 2 cm cubes
- 1/4 cup (60ml) olive oil
- 1 orange, zested and juiced
- 1 long red chilli, finely chopped
- 2 garlic cloves, crushed
- 4 Coles Australian Lamb Forequarter chops
- 3 spring onions, finely chopped
- 3/4 cup pearl couscous
- 1 1/2 cups (375ml) chicken stock
- 2 tablespoons dried cranberries
- 60g pkt Coles Brand Australian baby spinach
- 100g fetta, crumbled
- Orange slices, to serve
- Flat-leaf parsley sprigs, to serve

Direction

- Preheat oven to 180C. Place the pumpkin on a baking tray lined with baking paper. Drizzle with 2 tsp. olive oil. Season with salt and pepper. Bake in oven for 25-30 mins or until golden and cooked through.
- Meanwhile, combine the orange juice, orange zest, chili, garlic, and 2 tbsp. of the remaining olive oil. Place the lamb forequarter chops in a glass or ceramic dish. Pour over two-thirds of the marinade. Set aside for 15 mins to allow the flavors to develop.
- Heat remaining olive oil in a saucepan over medium-low heat. Add the spring onion and cook for 2 mins. Add the couscous and stir for 1 min. Add the stock and bring to the boil. Reduce heat to low. Cook, covered, for 10 mins or until most of the liquid has evaporated. Remove from heat and set aside for 10 mins to rest.
- Heat a barbecue or chargrill plate on medium-high heat. Cook lamb chops for 3 mins each side or until cooked to your liking. Transfer to a plate, cover with foil and set aside for 5 mins to rest.
- Combine the pumpkin, couscous, dried cranberries, spinach, feta and remaining orange juice mixture. Divide chops among serving plates. Top with sliced orange and parsley sprigs. Serve with the couscous salad.

31. Chinese Lamb With Ginger Sauce

Serving: 0 | Prep: 20mins | Ready in: 40mins

Ingredients

- 1 teaspoon Szechuan peppercorns (see note)
- 2 cinnamon quills, broken
- 2 wide strips mandarin or orange zest, finely chopped
- 80ml (1/3 cup) dark soy sauce
- 2 tablespoons Chinese rice wine (shaoxing - see note)
- 4 spring onions, finely chopped
- 4cm piece ginger, grated
- 2 tablespoons peanut oil
- 16 lamb cutlets, French-trimmed
- 1/2 long red chilli, seeded, finely chopped (see note)
- 1/4 cup coriander leaves
- 1 spring onion, thinly sliced on the diagonal
- Lime wedges, to serve
- 1 1/2 tablespoons vegetable oil
- 4cm piece ginger, finely grated
- 2 cloves garlic, crushed
- 2 tablespoons caster sugar
- 1 1/2 tablespoons light soy sauce
- 1 1/2 tablespoons Chinese rice wine (shaoxing - see note)
- 1 1/2 tablespoons Chinese black vinegar (see note)

Direction

- To marinate lamb, heat a small frying pan over medium heat. Add peppercorns and cinnamon, and cook, stirring, for 1 minute or until fragrant. Add zest, dark soy sauce, rice wine, spring onions, ginger and oil, and bring to a simmer. Place lamb in a bowl, then pour over marinade. Turn lamb to coat, then stand at room temperature for 10 minutes to marinate.
- Meanwhile, to make sauce, heat oil in a small saucepan over low–medium heat. Add ginger and garlic, and stir for 2 minutes. Stir in sugar, light soy sauce, rice wine, vinegar and 125ml (1/2 cup) water. Bring to a simmer, then cook for 2 minutes, stirring to dissolve sugar.
- Drain lamb, discarding marinade. Heat a large frying pan over medium heat. Cook lamb, in 2 batches, for 1 1/2 minutes each side or until browned. Return all lamb to pan. Add sauce and bring to a simmer, turning to coat lamb in sauce.
- Transfer lamb to a platter. Spoon sauce from pan into a small bowl. Scatter lamb with chili, coriander and spring onion. Serve with sauce and lime wedges.

32. Chutney And Rosemary Lamb Chops

Serving: 4 | Prep: 10mins | Ready in: 47mins

Ingredients

- 2 tablespoons olive oil
- 12 (100g each) lamb loin chops, trimmed
- 1 brown onion, sliced
- 1/2 cup dry white wine
- 250g jar fruit chutney
- 1 cup Italian tomato passata sauce
- 1 cup Massel chicken style liquid stock
- 2 teaspoons chopped rosemary leaves
- 1 cup frozen peas
- cooked risoni pasta, to serve

Direction

- Heat one tablespoon of oil in a large, non-stick frying pan over medium-high heat. Cook lamb, in batches, for 2 to 3 minutes each side or until browned. Remove to a plate. Cover with foil and set aside.
- Reduce heat to medium. Add onion to pan. Cook, stirring occasionally, for 3 minutes. Add wine. Cook for 1 minute or until liquid has nearly evaporated. Add chutney, passata, stock and rosemary. Season with salt and pepper. Reduce heat to low. Simmer, uncovered, stirring occasionally, for 10 minutes or until sauce thickens.
- Return lamb to pan with peas. Cook for a further 5 minutes or until lamb is heated through and peas are tender. Serve with risoni.

Nutrition Information

- Calories: 1058.531 calories
- Sugar: 31 grams sugar
- Protein: 76 grams protein
- Cholesterol: 210 milligrams cholesterol
- Sodium: 1003.16 milligrams sodium
- Total Fat: 66 grams fat
- Saturated Fat: 27 grams saturated fat
- Total Carbohydrate: 35 grams carbohydrates

33. Classic Crumbed Cutlets

Serving: 4 | Prep: 40mins | Ready in: 75mins

Ingredients

- 12 (480g) lamb cutlets, French trimmed
- 2 cups fresh breadcrumbs
- 1 tablespoon fresh flat-leaf parsley leaves, finely chopped
- 1/4 cup plain flour
- 2 eggs, lightly beaten
- Vegetable oil, for shallow-frying
- Steamed peas, to serve

- Gravy, to serve
- Lemon wedges, to serve
- 800g cream delight potatoes, peeled, chopped
- 40g butter
- 1/2 cup milk

Direction

- Make fluffy mashed potato: Place potato in a large saucepan. Cover with cold water. Bring to the boil over high heat. Boil for 12 to 15 minutes or until potato is very tender. Drain. Using back of a wooden spoon, push potato through a fine sieve over a bowl. Add butter and milk. Season with salt and pepper. Stir to combine.
- Using the heel of your hand, gently flatten meat on each cutlet.
- Combine breadcrumbs and parsley on a plate. Place flour on another plate. Whisk egg and 1 tablespoon cold water in a shallow bowl. One at a time, coat each cutlet in flour, shaking off excess. Dip in egg. Press in breadcrumbs. Place on a plate. Cover with plastic wrap. Refrigerate for 20 minutes.
- Pour oil into a large frying pan to cover base. Heat over medium heat. Cook cutlets, in batches, for 5 minutes each side for medium or until cooked to your liking. Transfer to a plate lined with paper towel.
- Serve cutlets with Fluffy mashed potato, peas, gravy and lemon wedges.

Nutrition Information

- Calories: 688.559 calories
- Total Carbohydrate: 55.5 grams carbohydrates
- Total Fat: 34.3 grams fat
- Saturated Fat: 12.3 grams saturated fat
- Protein: 35.2 grams protein
- Cholesterol: 173 milligrams cholesterol
- Sodium: 575 milligrams sodium

34. Coriander Lamb With Roasted Carrots And Quinoa

Serving: 4 | Prep: 15mins | Ready in: 55mins

Ingredients

- 2 tbs extra virgin olive oil
- 2 tsp ground coriander
- 2 tsp finely grated lemon rind
- 1 garlic clove, crushed
- 1 bunch Dutch carrots or 200g baby carrots, peeled, halved lengthways
- 1 cup (200g) white quinoa
- 4 Coles Australian Lamb Forequarter Chops
- 180g haloumi, thinly sliced
- 1/4 cup (35g) hazelnuts, toasted, chopped
- 2 tbs lemon juice
- 1 tbs extra virgin olive oil, extra
- 1/3 cup mint leaves
- Lemon zest, to serve
- Lemon halves, to serve

Direction

- Preheat oven to 180°C. Combine oil, coriander, lemon rind and garlic in a small jug. Place carrots on a greased baking tray and pour over half the garlic mixture. Toss to coat. Bake for 30 mins or until carrots are tender.
- Meanwhile, combine the quinoa and 1½ cups (375ml) water in a saucepan over high heat. Bring to the boil. Cover and reduce heat to low. Simmer for 15 mins or until the liquid is absorbed and quinoa is tender. Set aside, covered, for 5 mins to steam. Use a fork to separate the grains.
- Place the lamb in a large glass or ceramic dish. Pour over the remaining garlic mixture and turn to coat. Preheat a barbecue grill or chargrill on high. Cook lamb for 3 mins each side for medium or until cooked to your liking. Transfer to a plate and cover with foil. Set aside for 5 minutes to rest.
- While the lamb is resting, cook the haloumi on grill for 2 mins each side or until charred. Cover to keep warm.

- Combine the quinoa, carrots, haloumi and hazelnut in a large bowl. Divide among serving plates with the lamb. Combine lemon juice and extra oil in a bowl. Drizzle over the salad on the plates. Season. Sprinkle with mint and lemon zest and serve with lemon halves.

35. Costolette D'agnello

Serving: 4 | Prep: 10mins | Ready in: 35mins

Ingredients

- 12 lamb cutlets, French trimmed
- 1 tablespoon olive oil
- 1 red onion, halved, thinly sliced
- 400g can diced tomatoes
- 250g Ausfresh Tuscan Antipasto mix, drained (see note)
- Fresh continental parsley leaves, to serve

Direction

- Use the flat side of a meat mallet to gently pound lamb until 1cm thick.
- Heat oil in a frying pan over high heat. Cook half the lamb for 2-3 minutes each side for medium rare or until cooked to your liking. Transfer to a plate. Repeat with remaining lamb.
- Reduce heat to medium. Cook the onion, stirring, for 5 minutes or until soft. Add the tomato and antipasto mix and cook, stirring occasionally, for 3 minutes or until heated through. Return lamb to pan and cook for 2 minutes or until heated through. Sprinkle with parsley to serve.

Nutrition Information

- Calories: 316.675 calories
- Saturated Fat: 11 grams saturated fat
- Protein: 25 grams protein
- Total Carbohydrate: 12 grams carbohydrates
- Total Fat: 18 grams fat

36. Crumbed Lamb Cutlets With Pasta Salad

Serving: 4 | Prep: 20mins | Ready in: 35mins

Ingredients

- 200g dried mini penne pasta
- 8 (600g) lamb cutlets, trimmed
- 1/4 cup vegetable oil
- 1/2 x 120g packet roasted garlic herb coating mix (we used McCormick brand)
- 250g cherry tomatoes, quartered
- 1 medium Lebanese cucumber, diced
- 2 celery stalks, diced
- 125g can corn kernels, drained
- 1/4 cup French dressing

Direction

- Cook pasta in a large saucepan of boiling, salted water, following packet directions, until tender. Drain.
- Meanwhile, using a meat mallet, flatten lamb cutlets until 1cm thick. Brush cutlets with 1 tablespoon oil. Press coating mix over cutlets.
- Heat a large frying pan over medium-low heat. Add 2 tablespoons oil. Cook lamb, in batches, for 2 to 3 minutes each side for medium, or until cooked to your liking. Cover to keep warm.
- Add tomato, cucumber, celery, corn and dressing to pasta. Toss to combine. Serve cutlets with pasta salad.

Nutrition Information

- Calories: 566.908 calories
- Cholesterol: 65 milligrams cholesterol
- Saturated Fat: 6.4 grams saturated fat
- Total Carbohydrate: 51.6 grams carbohydrates
- Protein: 28.5 grams protein
- Total Fat: 26.3 grams fat

- Sodium: 857 milligrams sodium

---

37. Crumbed Lamb Cutlets With Pumpkin Salad And Pesto

Serving: 4 | Prep: 25mins | Ready in: 50mins

Ingredients

- 600g Kent pumpkin, peeled, seeded, cut into 2.5cm pieces
- 1 red capsicum, thinly sliced
- 1 red onion, cut into wedges
- 1/3 cup (80ml) olive oil
- 1/4 cup (35g) plain flour
- 2 Coles Brand Australian Free Range Eggs, lightly whisked
- 2/3 cup (70g) dried breadcrumbs
- 1/4 cup (20g) finely grated parmesan
- 8 Coles Australian Lamb Cutlets, French-trimmed
- 120g baby rocket leaves
- 2 x 125g cans chickpeas, drained, rinsed
- 2 tablespoons balsamic dressing
- 1/3 cup (90g) Coles Gourmet Basil Pesto

Direction

- Preheat oven to 220C. Line a baking tray with baking paper. Place the pumpkin, capsicum and onion on the tray and drizzle with 1 tbsp. of the oil. Bake for 25 mins or until golden and tender.
- Meanwhile, place flour on a plate. Place egg in a shallow bowl. Combine breadcrumbs and parmesan on a plate. Coat 1 cutlet in flour and shake off excess. Dip in egg and then in breadcrumb mixture. Place on a plate. Repeat with remaining flour, egg, breadcrumb mixture and lamb.
- Heat remaining oil in a large frying pan over medium-high heat. Add lamb and cook for 2-3 mins each side for medium or until cooked to your liking. Transfer to a plate and set aside for 5 mins to rest.
- Combine pumpkin, capsicum, onion, rocket, chickpeas and dressing in a large bowl and gently toss to combine. Divide pumpkin salad and lamb among serving plates and top with pesto to serve.

---

38. Crumbed Lamb Cutlets With Roast Greek Salad Vegetables

Serving: 4 | Prep: 0S | Ready in:

Ingredients

- 1 red onion, cut into thin wedges
- 3 roma tomatoes, halved
- 2 red capsicums, roughly chopped
- 3 zucchini, halved lengthways, thickly sliced
- 1 garlic clove, finely chopped
- 1/3 cup (80ml) olive oil
- 1 teaspoon dried oregano
- 200g feta, chopped
- 1/2 cup (80g) kalamata olives
- 1 tablespoon oregano leaves, plus extra to serve
- 1 cup (100g) dried breadcrumbs
- Grated zest of 1 lemon
- 8 French-trimmed lamb cutlets
- 1/4 cup (35g) plain flour, seasoned
- 1 egg, lightly beaten
- Lemon wedges, to serve

Direction

- Preheat the oven to 200°C and line a large baking tray with foil.
- Toss vegetables and garlic with 2 tablespoons oil and 1/2 teaspoon dried oregano. Season. Spread on the tray and bake for 15 minutes or until vegetables are just tender. Add feta, olives and oregano leaves and bake for a further 5-8 minutes until feta is golden.
- Meanwhile, combine crumbs with zest and remaining 1/2 teaspoon dried oregano, then season. Coat lamb first in flour, then in egg and crumbs, shaking off any excess.

- Heat remaining 2 tablespoons oil in a fry pan over medium-high heat. In batches, cook lamb for 2-3 minutes each side for medium-rare or until cooked to your liking. Place lamb cutlets on a serving platter with roasted vegetables, lemon wedges and oregano.

Nutrition Information

- Calories: 701.226 calories
- Saturated Fat: 16 grams saturated fat
- Cholesterol: 168 milligrams cholesterol
- Sodium: 1142.51 milligrams sodium
- Sugar: 6 grams sugar
- Protein: 40 grams protein
- Total Fat: 46 grams fat
- Total Carbohydrate: 29 grams carbohydrates

39. Crushed Peas And Potatoes With Sumac Lamb Cutlets

Serving: 4 | Prep: 10mins | Ready in: 35mins

Ingredients

- 12 (about 800g) lamb cutlets
- 1 tablespoon thyme leaves
- 1 tablespoon sesame seeds
- 2 teaspoons sumac
- 2 tablespoons olive oil
- 500g baby coliban (chat) or desiree potatoes
- 50g butter
- 2 garlic cloves, crushed
- 3 cups (450g) frozen peas

Direction

- Place cutlets in a bowl. Sprinkle with thyme, sesame seeds and sumac; drizzle with oil. Gently toss to combine. Place in fridge for 30 minutes to develop flavors.
- Place the potatoes in a large saucepan and cover with plenty of cold water. Place over high heat and bring to the boil. Reduce heat to medium and simmer for 10 minutes or until tender. Drain well. Place the potatoes on a clean work surface and cover with a clean tea towel. Use the palm of your hand to gently crush the potatoes. Return to the pan with half the butter and garlic over high heat and cook, shaking the pan, until well combined. Season with salt and pepper.
- Meanwhile heat a large frying pan over medium-high heat. Add the cutlets and cook for 2-3 minutes each side for medium or until cooked to your liking. Transfer to a plate and cover with foil. Set aside for 5 minutes to rest.
- Cook the peas in a large saucepan of boiling water for 2-3 minutes or until heated through. Drain well. Return the peas to the pan with the remaining butter and garlic and place over medium heat. Cook, shaking the pan occasionally, for 2 minutes or until well combined. Remove from heat. Use a potato masher or fork to lightly crush. Season with salt and pepper.
- Spoon the potato and peas among serving plates. Top with lamb cutlets and serve immediately.

Nutrition Information

- Calories: 657.728 calories
- Saturated Fat: 15 grams saturated fat
- Sugar: 7 grams sugar
- Cholesterol: 162 milligrams cholesterol
- Sodium: 208.99 milligrams sodium
- Total Fat: 39 grams fat
- Protein: 48 grams protein
- Total Carbohydrate: 24 grams carbohydrates

40. Cumin And Sesame Lamb With Silverbeet And Beetroot Salad

Serving: 4 | Prep: 15mins | Ready in: 25mins

Ingredients

- 2 teaspoons cumin seeds
- 2 teaspoons sesame seeds
- 2 tablespoon peanut oil
- 4 Coles Australian Lamb Forequarter Chops
- 4 silverbeet leaves
- 250g cooked beetroot, coarsely chopped
- 1/2 cup mint leaves
- 1 carrot, cut into long matchsticks
- 2 spring onions, sliced
- 1 tablespoon balsamic vinegar
- 2 teaspoons wholegrain mustard
- 80g fetta, crumbled
- Lemon wedges, to serve

Direction

- Combine cumin seeds, sesame seeds and 1 tablespoon oil in a large bowl. Add lamb and turn to coat. Season.
- Heat a chargrill or large frying pan on medium-high. Cook lamb for 2-3 mins each side or until cooked to your liking. Transfer to a plate. Cover with foil. Set aside for 5 mins to rest.
- Meanwhile, discard stem and centre vein from silverbeet. Shred leaves finely. Combine silverbeet in a large bowl with beetroot, mint, carrot and spring onion. Whisk vinegar, mustard and remaining oil in a small bowl and season. Add dressing to salad and toss to combine. Sprinkle with feta.
- Divide salad and lamb among serving plates. Serve with lemon wedges.

41. Cumin Lamb With Pumpkin Chickpea Pilaf

Serving: 4 | Prep: 15mins | Ready in: 65mins

Ingredients

- 750g Butternut pumpkin, peeled, seeded, cut into 2.5cm pieces
- Olive oil spray
- 1 tablespoon olive oil
- 1 brown onion, finely chopped
- 2 garlic cloves, crushed
- 2 teaspoons finely grated fresh ginger
- 300g (1 1/2 cups) Basmati rice
- 750ml (3 cups) Massel vegetable liquid stock
- 400g can chickpeas, rinsed, drained
- 150g baby spinach leaves
- 8 lamb cutlets
- 1 tablespoon ground cumin
- Fresh coriander leaves, to serve

Direction

- Preheat oven to 200°C. Line a baking tray with baking paper. Place pumpkin on tray. Spray with oil. Roast for 20 minutes or until tender.
- Meanwhile, heat oil in a saucepan over medium heat. Cook the onion, stirring, for 2 minutes or until softened slightly. Add garlic and ginger. Cook, stirring, for 1 minute or until aromatic. Add rice. Stir to coat. Add stock and chickpeas. Bring to boil. Reduce heat to low. Cover. Cook for 15 minutes or until tender. Stir in spinach. Cover and set aside for 2-3 minutes to steam. Use a fork to separate grains. Stir in pumpkin.
- Sprinkle the lamb with cumin. Spray a frying pan with oil. Cook the lamb over medium-high heat for 3 minutes each side or until cooked to your liking.
- Divide the pilaf and lamb among serving plates. Top with coriander.

Nutrition Information

- Calories: 690.232 calories
- Protein: 39 grams protein
- Cholesterol: 80 milligrams cholesterol
- Sodium: 960.99 milligrams sodium
- Total Fat: 19 grams fat
- Saturated Fat: 5 grams saturated fat
- Total Carbohydrate: 85 grams carbohydrates
- Sugar: 12 grams sugar

42. Curried Lamb Cutlets With Radish Yoghurt

Serving: 6 | Prep: 15mins | Ready in: 20mins

Ingredients

- 18 lamb cutlets, excess fat trimmed
- 1 1/2 tablespoons curry powder
- 1 garlic clove, crushed
- 1 tablespoon peanut oil
- Salt freshly ground black pepper
- 1 x 200g container natural yoghurt
- 6 radishes, washed, dried, stems and roots trimmed, cut into matchsticks
- 1/4 cup loosely packed finely chopped fresh coriander
- 2 green shallots, ends trimmed, finely chopped
- 1 tablespoon fresh lemon juice
- 1 garlic clove, crushed
- Pinch of salt

Direction

- Place cutlets in a large glass or ceramic dish. Combine curry powder, garlic and oil in a bowl. Pour over cutlets and turn to coat. Cover with plastic wrap and place in the fridge for 30 minutes to marinate.
- Meanwhile, to make the radish yoghurt, combine the yoghurt, radish, coriander, green shallot, lemon juice and garlic in a serving bowl. Taste and season with salt. Cover with plastic wrap and place in the fridge until required.
- Preheat a chargrill on medium-high. Drain cutlets and season with salt and pepper. Cook on grill for 2 minutes each side for medium or until cooked to your liking. Transfer to a serving platter and serve with the radish yoghurt.

Nutrition Information

- Calories: 355.393 calories
- Total Fat: 21 grams fat
- Total Carbohydrate: 4 grams carbohydrates
- Sugar: 3 grams sugar
- Protein: 37 grams protein
- Cholesterol: 126 milligrams cholesterol
- Saturated Fat: 8 grams saturated fat
- Sodium: 166.83 milligrams sodium

43. Curried Lamb With Rice Pilaf

Serving: 4 | Prep: 15mins | Ready in: 50mins

Ingredients

- 2 tablespoons sunflower oil
- 1 onion, thinly sliced
- 1/2 cup (140g) thick Greek-style yoghurt
- 2 tablespoons Madras curry paste (see note)
- 1 cup (200g) Basmati rice
- 1/4 cup chopped mint leaves, plus extra sprigs to serve
- 12 French-trimmed lamb cutlets
- 1/2 cup (40g) flaked almonds, lightly toasted

Direction

- Heat 1 tablespoon oil in a saucepan over medium-low heat and add the onion. Cook, stirring, for 5-6 minutes until softened. Remove half the onion with a slotted spoon and set aside. Add 1/4 cup (70g) yoghurt and 1 tablespoon curry paste to the pan and cook, stirring, for 2 minutes or until combined. Add the rice, stirring to coat the grains, then add 1 1/2 cups (375ml) cold water and increase heat to medium. Bring to the boil, then cover with a lid, reduce heat to low and cook for 25 minutes or until the liquid is absorbed and the rice is cooked. Remove from heat and stand, covered, for 5 minutes, then stir through the chopped mint and season.
- Meanwhile, heat remaining 1 tablespoon oil in a fry pan over medium-high heat and cook cutlets, in batches, for 2 minutes on each side. Brush each side with the remaining 1 tablespoon curry paste and cook for a further 1

minute on each side. Transfer the cutlets to a plate and rest, loosely covered with foil.
- To serve, spread the rice on a serving platter and top with lamb and reserved onions. Drizzle with the remaining 1/4 cup (70g) yoghurt, garnish with almonds and extra mint sprigs, and season.

Nutrition Information

- Calories: 683.779 calories
- Total Fat: 36 grams fat
- Protein: 42 grams protein
- Cholesterol: 126 milligrams cholesterol
- Sodium: 533.36 milligrams sodium
- Saturated Fat: 9 grams saturated fat
- Total Carbohydrate: 47 grams carbohydrates
- Sugar: 7 grams sugar

44. Dukkah Lamb Cutlets With Tomato And Spinach Salad

Serving: 4 | Prep: 20mins | Ready in: 50mins

Ingredients

- 1/3 cup dry-roasted hazelnuts
- 1 teaspoon ground cumin
- 1 tablespoon sesame seeds
- 1/3 cup wholemeal breadcrumbs
- 1 egg
- 8 (60g each) lamb cutlets
- 1 tablespoon olive oil
- 1 medium red onion, cut into thin wedges
- 2 teaspoons olive oil
- 250g cherry tomatoes
- 1 tablespoon French dressing
- 100g baby spinach

Direction

- Make tomato and spinach salad Preheat oven to 220°C/ 200°C fan-forced. Line a baking tray with baking paper. Place onion on prepared tray. Drizzle with oil. Bake for 15 to 20 minutes or until tender, adding tomatoes to tray for last 10 minutes. Remove from oven. Place in a bowl. Add dressing. Toss to combine.
- Meanwhile, process hazelnuts until they resemble fine breadcrumbs. Combine hazelnuts, cumin, sesame seeds and breadcrumbs on a plate. Lightly beat egg in a shallow bowl. Dip 1 cutlet in egg mixture, then hazelnut mixture. Place on a baking tray. Coat remaining cutlets.
- Heat oil in a frying pan over medium heat. Cook cutlets for 2 minutes each side for medium or until cooked to your liking. Add spinach to tomato mixture. Toss to coat. Serve cutlets with salad.

Nutrition Information

- Calories: 622.834 calories
- Protein: 24.9 grams protein
- Cholesterol: 145 milligrams cholesterol
- Saturated Fat: 20.1 grams saturated fat
- Total Carbohydrate: 6.2 grams carbohydrates
- Sodium: 223 milligrams sodium
- Total Fat: 55.3 grams fat

45. Dukkah Crusted Lamb Chops With Fruit And Nut Couscous

Serving: 4 | Prep: 10mins | Ready in: 18mins

Ingredients

- 50g pistachio dukkah
- 8 (about 600g) lamb loin chops
- 1 tablespoon olive oil
- 250g couscous
- 55g (1/3 cup) finely chopped mixed dried fruit
- 250ml (1 cup) boiling water
- 40g (1/4 cup) pistachio kernels, coarsely chopped
- 1 1/2 teaspoons vegetable salt (see note)
- 1/2 teaspoon chilli powder

- 1 tablespoon pistachio dukkah, extra
- 1 bunch rocket, ends trimmed
- 1/2 cup fresh coriander leaves
- 70g (1/4 cup) Tamar Valley Greek Style Yoghurt

Direction

- Place the dukkah on a plate. Press both sides of the lamb into the dukkah to coat. Heat the oil in a large frying pan over medium-high heat. Add the lamb and cook for 4 minutes each side for medium or until cooked to your liking.
- Meanwhile, place the couscous and dried fruit in a large heatproof bowl. Add the boiling water. Cover and set aside for 2 minutes or until all the liquid is absorbed. Use a fork to separate the grains. Stir in the pistachio, vegetable salt, chilli powder and extra dukkah.
- Divide the couscous mixture, rocket and lamb among serving plates. Top with the coriander. Serve with the yoghurt.

Nutrition Information

- Calories: 731.34 calories
- Protein: 45 grams protein
- Total Fat: 35 grams fat
- Saturated Fat: 11 grams saturated fat
- Total Carbohydrate: 56 grams carbohydrates

46. Easy Braised Lettuce And Peas With Lamb

Serving: 0 | Prep: 10mins | Ready in: 30mins

Ingredients

- 20g butter
- 2 tablespoons olive oil
- 1 leek, trimmed, halved, washed, sliced
- 2 garlic cloves, crushed
- 1 cup Massel chicken style liquid stock
- 1/2 cup frozen peas
- 1/2 iceberg lettuce, cut into thin wedges
- 1 tablespoon roughly chopped fresh mint leaves
- 4 (980g total) lamb forequarter chops, trimmed
- Crusty bread, to serve

Direction

- Heat butter and 1 tablespoon oil in a large, non-stick frying pan over medium heat until butter has melted. Add leek. Cook for 3 to 4 minutes or until softened but not browned. Add garlic. Cook for 1 minute or until fragrant.
- Add stock. Bring to the boil. Add peas. Return to the boil. Reduce heat to low. Add lettuce. Cook for 2 minutes or until lettuce just starts to wilt. Season with salt and pepper. Sprinkle with mint.
- Meanwhile, heat a chargrill pan over medium-high heat. Drizzle lamb with remaining oil and season with salt and pepper. Cook for 3 to 4 minutes each side, for medium or until cooked to your liking. Transfer to a plate. Cover. Rest for 5 minutes.
- Serve braised lettuce with lamb chops and crusty bread.

Nutrition Information

- Calories: 532.731 calories
- Total Carbohydrate: 25.6 grams carbohydrates
- Cholesterol: 97 milligrams cholesterol
- Sodium: 815 milligrams sodium
- Total Fat: 31.2 grams fat
- Saturated Fat: 9.8 grams saturated fat
- Protein: 37.4 grams protein

47. Fennel And Chilli Spiced Lamb Chops With Superfood Vegetable Mix

Serving: 4 | Prep: 10mins | Ready in: 20mins

Ingredients

- 1 tablespoon olive oil
- 1 tablespoon lemon juice
- 1 tablespoon red wine vinegar
- 2 teaspoons fennel seeds
- 1 red chilli, chopped
- 1 garlic clove, crushed
- 2 teaspoons ground paprika
- 1/2 teaspoon sea salt flakes
- 8 Coles Lamb Loin Chops
- 2 tablespoons olive oil, extra
- 350g pkt Coles Superfood Vegetable Mix
- 2 garlic cloves, extra, crushed
- Thinly sliced red chilli, to serve
- Lemon wedges, to serve

Direction

- Blend or process oil, lemon juice, vinegar, fennel seeds, chopped chili, garlic, paprika and salt in a blender or food processor until almost smooth. Transfer to a shallow ceramic dish. Add lamb and turn to coat.
- Preheat a barbecue grill or chargrill on high. Cook the lamb for 3-4 mins each side for medium or until cooked to your liking. Transfer to a plate and cover with foil. Set aside for 5 mins to rest.
- Meanwhile, heat extra oil in a wok or large frying pan over high heat. Stir-fry vegetable mix and extra garlic about 2 mins or until vegetables have just wilted. Season.
- Serve lamb and vegetables with sliced chili and lemon wedges.

48. Feta And Semi Dried Tomato Crusted Lamb

Serving: 2 | Prep: 30mins | Ready in: 75mins

Ingredients

- 40g semi-dried tomatoes, finely chopped
- 40g feta cheese, crumbled
- 1/4 cup fresh white breadcrumbs
- 2 teaspoons pinenuts
- 2 tablespoons thyme leaves
- 1 egg yolk
- 2 x 3-cutlet racks of lamb, trimmed
- 1 sebago potato, peeled, cut into 2cm cubes
- 1 carrot, peeled, cut into 2cm cubes
- 1 sweet potato, peeled, cut into 2cm cubes
- 200g piece Jap pumpkin, peeled, cut into 2cm cubes
- 2 tablespoons olive oil
- dressed salad leaves, to serve

Direction

- Preheat oven to 200°C. Combine semi-dried tomato, feta, breadcrumbs, pine nuts, 2 teaspoons thyme leaves, egg yolk and salt and pepper in a bowl. Using clean hands, mix until well combined. Place lamb racks on a chopping board.
- Coat each lamb rack in breadcrumb mixture, pressing on with fingertips. Place racks, interlocking cutlet bones, in the centre of a greased roasting pan.
- Combine potato, carrot, sweet potato, pumpkin, oil, remaining thyme leaves and salt and pepper in a large bowl. Toss to coat. Spoon vegetables around edge of roasting pan. Roast for 25 to 30 minutes for medium lamb or until cooked to your liking. Transfer lamb racks to a plate. Cover. Stand for 10 minutes. Increase oven temperature to 250°C. Roast vegetables for a further 8 minutes or until golden and crisp.
- Cut lamb racks into cutlets. Serve with vegetables and salad leaves.

Nutrition Information

- Calories: 949.308 calories
- Saturated Fat: 24 grams saturated fat
- Sugar: 19 grams sugar
- Sodium: 408.63 milligrams sodium
- Total Fat: 66 grams fat
- Total Carbohydrate: 38 grams carbohydrates
- Protein: 47 grams protein
- Cholesterol: 206 milligrams cholesterol

49. Fresh Minted Peas With Spring Lamb

Serving: 4 | Prep: 15mins | Ready in: 85mins

Ingredients

- 1kg Kent/Jap pumpkin, deseeded, cut into large chunks
- 1 tablespoon olive oil
- 12 lamb cutlets
- 2 cups (300g) shelled fresh peas
- 250g sugar snap peas
- 1/3 cup mint leaves
- 1 red onion, halved

Direction

- Preheat oven to 210°C. Place pumpkin chunks onto a baking tray. Drizzle with 1 tablespoon olive oil and season. Bake for 45 minutes.
- In batches, cook 12 lamb cutlets in a frying pan over a medium-high heat for 3-4 minutes each side. Transfer to a plate and cover. Add red onion sliced to the pan and cook until soft.
- Boil shelled fresh peas and sugar snap peas in water for 3-4 minutes. Toss through mint leaves. Serve with the pumpkin, onion and lamb.

Nutrition Information

- Calories: 489.95 calories

- Sodium: 116.39 milligrams sodium
- Cholesterol: 121 milligrams cholesterol
- Total Fat: 21 grams fat
- Saturated Fat: 7 grams saturated fat
- Total Carbohydrate: 25 grams carbohydrates
- Sugar: 19 grams sugar
- Protein: 44 grams protein

50. Garlicky Lamb Chops With Barbecued Green Beans

Serving: 4 | Prep: 10mins | Ready in: 25mins

Ingredients

- 1/3 cup extra-virgin olive oil, divided
- 2 garlic cloves, finely chopped
- 2 tablespoons fresh oregano, coarsely chopped
- 8 lamb loin chops (about 120g each)
- 400g green beans, trimmed
- 250g vine ripened cherry tomatoes, halved
- Lemon wedges, for serving

Direction

- Prepare a barbecue for medium-high heat. In a medium bowl, whisk 1/4 cup of the oil, garlic, oregano, 1/2 teaspoon of sea salt flakes and 1/4 teaspoon of freshly ground black pepper.
- Coat the lamb chops with 2 tablespoons of the oregano dressing and season with salt and pepper. Set the remaining oregano dressing aside. Place the chops on the barbecue grates, close the hood and cook for about 3 minutes, or until well browned on the bottom. Turn the chops over, close the hood and cook for about 3 minutes, or until an instant-read thermometer inserted into the center of the lamb chops reaches 54°C. Transfer the chops to a plate to rest for 5 minutes.
- Meanwhile, in a large bowl, toss the beans with the remaining 1 tablespoon of oil and season with salt. Place a barbecue tray or wire rack over the hottest part of the barbecue. Working in batches, place the beans on the

wire rack and cook, turning as needed, for about 3 minutes, or until the beans are lightly charred and tender. Transfer the beans to a bowl and toss with the tomatoes and remaining oregano dressing. Season to taste with salt and pepper.
- Serve the lamb chops on a platter with the vegetables and lemon wedges on the side.

- Sugar: 12.8 grams sugar
- Cholesterol: 180 milligrams cholesterol
- Sodium: 178 milligrams sodium
- Total Fat: 15.7 grams fat
- Total Carbohydrate: 47.2 grams carbohydrates
- Protein: 63 grams protein

51. Greek Lamb And Vegie Tray Bake

Serving: 4 | Prep: 5mins | Ready in: 70mins

Ingredients

- 6 baby potatoes, washed, quartered if large
- Extra virgin olive oil spray
- 8 Coles lamb loin chops, trimmed
- 1 red onion, halved, cut into wedges
- 2 medium red capsicums, cut into large pieces
- 275g Coles amoroso truss tomatoes
- 250g pkt Coles Brand Greek lemon, garlic herb marinade
- 150g green beans, steamed

Direction

- Preheat oven to 180C or 160C fan. Place the potatoes in a roasting pan and spray with oil. Roast for 15 mins.
- Meanwhile, heat a non-stick frying pan over medium-high heat. Sear the lamb for 1-2 mins each side or until golden.
- Add lamb, onion, capsicum and tomatoes to the potatoes. Pour over the marinade. Toss to combine. Roast for 45 mins or until potatoes are golden and lamb is tender. Serve with beans.

Nutrition Information

- Calories: 573.839 calories
- Saturated Fat: 5.4 grams saturated fat

52. Greek Vegetable And Lamb Tray Bake

Serving: 4 | Prep: 35mins | Ready in: 75mins

Ingredients

- 1 1/2 tablespoons fresh rosemary leaves
- 1 lemon, rind finely grated, juiced
- 60ml (1/4 cup) extra virgin olive oil
- 3 garlic cloves, crushed
- 2 teaspoons Masterfoods Oregano Leaves, plus extra, to serve
- 12 lamb cutlets, French trimmed
- 4 small (about 250g) potatoes, thinly sliced
- 2 small zucchini, cut into 5mm slices
- 1 large red capsicum, deseeded, coarsely chopped
- 1 brown onion, thinly sliced into rings
- 55g (1/3 cup) kalamata olives, pitted
- 100g Greek feta, coarsely crumbled
- Baby herbs, to serve (optional)

Direction

- Preheat the oven to 230°C/210°C fan forced and grease a large, shallow non-stick baking tray.
- Finely chop 1 tbsp. of the rosemary leaves. Combine the chopped rosemary, lemon rind, 1 tbsp. juice, 1 tbsp. oil, 2 garlic cloves and 1 tsp. dried oregano in a bowl. Add the lamb. Season, then toss to combine. Set aside to marinate.
- Place the potato, zucchini, capsicum and onion on the prepared tray and add 1 tbsp. lemon juice and the remaining rosemary, oil, garlic

and oregano. Season. Toss to combine. Bake for 30 minutes or until golden and tender.
- Meanwhile, heat a large non-stick frying pan over medium-high heat. Cook the lamb, turning, for 2-3 minutes or until browned.
- Top the vegetables with lamb, olives and feta. Bake for a further 5 minutes or until the lamb is cooked to your liking. Sprinkle with the extra oregano and baby herbs, if using.

Nutrition Information

- Calories: 473.698 calories
- Total Fat: 33 grams fat
- Protein: 31 grams protein
- Saturated Fat: 10 grams saturated fat
- Total Carbohydrate: 11 grams carbohydrates

53. Green Masala Lamb Cutlets

Serving: 6 | Prep: 360mins | Ready in: 365mins

Ingredients

- 1 teaspoon fennel seeds
- 1 teaspoon coriander seeds
- 1 teaspoon cardamom seeds (or 6-8 green cardamom pods, crushed)
- 1 cup coriander leaves, plus extra to garnish
- 1 cup mint leaves, plus extra to garnish
- 1 teaspoon chilli powder
- 1 teaspoon ground turmeric
- 1 1/2 teaspoons garam masala spice blend
- Juice of 1 lemon
- 2 tablespoons natural yoghurt, plus extra to serve
- 12 French-trimmed lamb cutlets

Direction

- Toast fennel, coriander and cardamom seeds in a dry fry pan over medium heat, stirring, for 1 minute or until fragrant. Place in a food processor with the herbs, remaining spices, juice and yoghurt and process to a paste. Transfer the paste to a dish with the lamb and turn to coat well in the mixture. Cover with plastic wrap and marinate in the fridge for at least 4 hours, preferably overnight.
- Heat a chargrill pan or barbecue on medium-high heat. Add lamb and cook for 2 minutes each side until charred but still pink in the centre, or longer to your liking.
- Garnish the lamb with extra herbs and serve with the tomato and spinach salad.

Nutrition Information

- Calories: 207.213 calories
- Total Fat: 11 grams fat
- Total Carbohydrate: 2 grams carbohydrates
- Sugar: 1 grams sugar
- Protein: 24 grams protein
- Cholesterol: 82 milligrams cholesterol
- Sodium: 84.71 milligrams sodium
- Saturated Fat: 4 grams saturated fat

54. Green Olive Lamb With White Bean Puree

Serving: 4 | Prep: 15mins | Ready in: 30mins

Ingredients

- 200g cherry truss tomatoes
- 2 medium zucchini, cut into 6cm long wedges
- Olive oil cooking spray
- 2 tablespoons extra virgin olive oil
- 8 lamb loin chops, fat trimmed
- 1/2 cup green olive tapenade (see Notes)
- 2 x 420g cans cannellini beans, drained, rinsed
- 1 garlic clove, quartered
- 2 tablespoons lemon juice
- 80g baby rocket
- 1 tablespoon balsamic vinegar
- Lemon zest, to serve

Direction

- Preheat oven to 200C/180C fan-forced. Line a baking tray with baking paper.
- Using scissors, cut tomatoes into 4 portions, leaving stems attached. Place tomatoes and zucchini on prepared tray. Spray with oil. Season with salt and pepper. Bake for 12 to 15 minutes or until vegetables are just tender. 3
- Meanwhile, heat 2 teaspoons oil in a large frying pan. Cook lamb, brushing with 1/3 cup of tapenade, for 3 minutes each side for medium or until cooked to your liking. Transfer to a plate. Cover loosely with foil. Set aside for 5 minutes to rest.
- Process beans and garlic in a food processor until smooth. With motor running, add lemon juice, 1 tablespoon remaining oil and 1 tablespoon cold water. Process to combine.
- Combine remaining tapenade and oil in a small bowl. Combine zucchini, rocket and vinegar in a medium bowl. Toss to combine. Serve lamb on white bean puree with a dollop of tapenade dressing. Sprinkle with lemon zest and serve with tomatoes and salad.

Nutrition Information

- Calories: 597.5 calories
- Total Carbohydrate: 27.5 grams carbohydrates
- Protein: 55.6 grams protein
- Cholesterol: 125 milligrams cholesterol
- Sodium: 745 milligrams sodium
- Total Fat: 28.6 grams fat
- Saturated Fat: 7.3 grams saturated fat

55. Grilled Lamb Cutlets With Olives, Mint And White Bean Puree

Serving: 6 | Prep: 25mins | Ready in: 35mins

Ingredients

- 2 tablespoons currants or sultanas
- 12 French-trimmed lamb cutlets
- 1 teaspoon dried oregano
- 1/4 cup (60ml) extra virgin olive oil
- 2 tablespoons lemon juice
- 2 tablespoons toasted pine nuts
- 2 tablespoons pitted kalamata olives, quartered
- 1 tablespoon salted capers, rinsed, drained
- 2 tablespoons mint leaves, finely chopped, plus extra leaves to serve
- 2 x 400g cans cannellini beans, rinsed, drained
- 1/4 cup (60ml) low-fat milk
- 1 tablespoon lemon juice
- 1 garlic clove, crushed
- 1/2 teaspoon paprika, plus extra to sprinkle
- 1 tablespoon extra virgin olive oil

Direction

- Soak currants or sultanas in hot water for 10 minutes. Drain and set aside.
- Meanwhile, for the bean puree, place the beans and milk in a saucepan over medium heat. Cook, stirring, for 2 minutes or until just below boiling point. Cool slightly, then transfer to a blender or food processor and whiz for 2 minutes until smooth and light. Add lemon juice, garlic, paprika, 2 teaspoons olive oil and some salt and pepper, then whiz for 1 minute or until combined. Set aside.
- Preheat a lightly oiled chargrill pan or barbecue to medium-high. Season lamb and scatter with oregano. Grill for 2-3 minutes until charred. Turn and cook for 2 minutes until pink in the center (or until cooked to your liking). Rest, loosely covered with foil, for 5 minutes.
- Meanwhile, whisk together oil, lemon juice, nuts, olives, capers, mint and soaked currants. Season and set aside.
- Drizzle lamb with dressing, then garnish with mint leaves. Spoon bean puree into a bowl, sprinkle with paprika, drizzle with remaining oil, then serve with the lamb.

Nutrition Information

- Calories: 464.138 calories

- Sodium: 357.28 milligrams sodium
- Total Fat: 28 grams fat
- Saturated Fat: 7 grams saturated fat
- Protein: 31 grams protein
- Cholesterol: 86 milligrams cholesterol
- Total Carbohydrate: 21 grams carbohydrates
- Sugar: 4 grams sugar

56. Haloumi Lamb Cutlets With Greek Potato Parcels

Serving: 4 | Prep: 25mins | Ready in: 50mins

Ingredients

- 750g baby potatoes, halved
- 250g mixed baby tomatoes
- 1 red onion, cut into wedges
- 95g (1/2 cup) mixed marinated olives
- 4 garlic cloves, bruised
- 1 lemon, rind finely grated, halved
- 8 sprigs fresh oregano
- 100ml extra virgin olive oil
- 125g day-old sourdough bread, torn
- 75g haloumi, coarsely grated
- 50g (1/3 cup) plain flour
- 2 eggs, lightly whisked
- 12 French-trimmed lamb cutlets
- Steamed green beans, to serve

Direction

- Preheat oven to 200C/180C fan forced. Microwave potatoes in a microwave-safe bowl on High for 5 minutes, until just tender. Drain liquid.
- Combine potato, tomatoes, onion, olives, garlic, lemon rind, 1 tbsp. juice, 4 oregano sprigs and 2 tbsp. oil in a bowl. Season. Divide among four squares of baking paper. Gather up the corners and scrunch together. Secure with kitchen string. Place on a baking tray. Bake for 20-25 minutes or until potatoes are tender.
- Meanwhile, process bread, halloumi and remaining oregano until finely chopped. Transfer to a plate. Place flour on a separate plate. Season. Place egg in a shallow bowl. Dip lamb in flour, then egg, then crumb mixture, pressing to coat.
- Heat 2 tbsp. oil in a large non-stick frying pan over medium heat. Cook 6 cutlets, turning, for 6 minutes or until cooked to your liking. Transfer to a plate. Repeat with remaining oil and cutlets. Serve with the potato parcels, beans and remaining lemon.

Nutrition Information

- Calories: 182.357 calories
- Saturated Fat: 10 grams saturated fat
- Total Carbohydrate: 53 grams carbohydrates
- Protein: 38 grams protein
- Total Fat: 42 grams fat

57. Herb Crusted Lamb Cutlets With Tomato Chutney

Serving: 8 | Prep: 15mins | Ready in: 35mins

Ingredients

- 1/2 cup fresh parsley, chopped
- 1/4 cup fresh mint, chopped
- 1/4 cup oil
- 1 tablespoon cajun seasoning
- 2 teaspoons thyme leaves, chopped
- 8 lamb cutlets, French trimmed
- 2 teaspoons olive oil
- 1 onion, thinly sliced
- 1 garlic clove, crushed
- 400g can tomatoes
- 1/4 cup brown sugar
- 1 tablespoon cider vinegar

Direction

- In a large bowl, combine parsley, mint, oil, seasoning and thyme. Season to taste. Add cutlets, turning to coat. Set aside.
- To make the tomato chutney, heat oil in a saucepan on high. Sauté onion and garlic for 4-5 mins until onion is tender. Add tomatoes, sugar and vinegar. Reduce heat to low and simmer, stirring, for 12-15 mins until thickened. Season to taste.
- Meanwhile, heat a char-grill or barbecue on high. Char-grill cutlets for 2-3 mins on each side, or until cooked to taste. Serve with tomato chutney.

lamb is cooked to your liking and potatoes are crisp. Cover lamb with foil. Set aside for 10 minutes to rest. Cut in half. Serve with the potatoes.

Nutrition Information

- Calories: 562.367 calories
- Total Carbohydrate: 45 grams carbohydrates
- Protein: 34 grams protein
- Cholesterol: 88 milligrams cholesterol
- Sodium: 182.91 milligrams sodium
- Total Fat: 26 grams fat
- Saturated Fat: 7 grams saturated fat
- Sugar: 3 grams sugar

58. Herb Crusted Lamb With Crisp Potatoes

Serving: 2 | Prep: 20mins | Ready in: 80mins

Ingredients

- 600g Baby Cream Delight potatoes
- 1 1/2 tablespoons olive oil
- 25g fresh breadcrumbs
- 2 tablespoons chopped fresh continental parsley
- 2 teaspoons finely grated lemon rind
- 1 garlic clove, crushed
- 1 lamb rack (6 cutlets), French-trimmed

Direction

- Preheat oven to 200°C. Cook the potatoes in a large saucepan of salted boiling water for 15 minutes or until tender. Drain. Place potatoes in a roasting pan. Use a potato masher to lightly crush the potatoes. Drizzle over 1 tablespoon of oil. Season with salt. Bake for 15 minutes.
- Meanwhile, combine the breadcrumbs, parsley, lemon rind, garlic and remaining oil in a bowl. Season. Press the breadcrumb mixture firmly onto the lamb.
- Add lamb to the roasting pan. Bake with the potatoes for 25-30 minutes for medium or until

59. Honey Sesame Lamb Cutlets

Serving: 4 | Prep: 20mins | Ready in: 30mins

Ingredients

- 1/4 cup honey
- 1/4 cup tamari
- 1 tablespoon sriracha chilli sauce, plus extra to serve
- 1 garlic clove, crushed
- 2 teaspoons sesame oil
- 1 teaspoon sesame seeds
- 1 tablespoon vegetable oil
- 12 lamb cutlets, French trimmed
- 1 tablespoon rice wine vinegar
- 2 baby gem lettuce, cut into wedges
- 2 Lebanese cucumbers, halved lengthways, thinly sliced diagonally
- 2 carrots, halved lengthways, thinly sliced diagonally
- 1 cup shredded red cabbage
- 2 spring onions, thinly sliced diagonally
- 2 long red chillies, thinly sliced diagonally
- Japanese-style mayonnaise, to serve

Direction

- Combine honey, tamari, chili sauce, garlic, sesame oil and sesame seeds in a medium jug. Set aside.
- Heat vegetable oil in a large frying pan over medium-high heat. Add lamb. Cook for 2 minutes each side or until browned. Add 2/3 of the honey mixture. Cook for a further 2 minutes or until sauce thickens and lamb is coated in sauce.
- Stir vinegar into remaining honey mixture. Place lettuce, cucumber, carrot and cabbage onto a serving tray. Drizzle with honey mixture. Top with lamb. Sprinkle with onion and chili. Serve with extra chili sauce and mayonnaise.

60. Indian Spiced Lamb Chops With Curried Spinach And Currant Pilaf

Serving: 4 | Prep: 15mins | Ready in: 40mins

Ingredients

- 3 teaspoons ground cumin
- 3 teaspoons garam marsala
- 1/2 teaspoon ground turmeric
- 12 (900g total) lamb loin chops
- Olive oil cooking spray
- Tamar Valley Greek Style Yoghurt, to serve
- Lime wedges, to serve
- 2 teaspoons olive oil
- 1 brown onion, halved, thinly sliced
- 2 tablespoons mild curry paste
- 1 1/2 cups Basmati rice
- 2 1/2 cups salt-reduced chicken stock
- 1 1/2 cups baby spinach
- 1/2 cup currants

Direction

- Make Curried spinach and currant pilaf: Heat oil in a saucepan over medium-high heat. Add onion. Cook, stirring, for 5 minutes or until softened. Add curry paste. Cook, stirring, for 1 to 2 minutes or until fragrant. Add rice. Stir to coat. Add stock. Bring to the boil. Reduce heat to low. Cover. Cook for 12 to 15 minutes or until rice is just tender and stock has absorbed. Stir in spinach and currants. Cover. Set aside for 5 minutes.
- Meanwhile, preheat barbecue chargrill on medium-high heat. Combine cumin, garam marsala and turmeric in a small bowl. Place chops on a chopping board. Sprinkle both sides with cumin mixture. Spray with oil. Cook for 3 to 4 minutes each side for medium or until cooked to your liking. Transfer to a rack over a baking tray. Cover loosely with foil. Set aside to rest for 5 minutes. Serve with pilaf, yoghurt and lime wedges.

Nutrition Information

- Calories: 702.182 calories
- Total Carbohydrate: 80.5 grams carbohydrates
- Cholesterol: 105 milligrams cholesterol
- Total Fat: 22.7 grams fat
- Saturated Fat: 8.4 grams saturated fat
- Protein: 41.4 grams protein
- Sodium: 919 milligrams sodium

61. Irish Stew

Serving: 4 | Prep: 20mins | Ready in: 160mins

Ingredients

- 1/4 cup plain flour
- 1.2kg lamb forequarter chops, trimmed
- 1/4 cup olive oil
- 1 brown onion, finely chopped
- 2 celery stalks, chopped
- 2 carrots, peeled, cut into 2cm pieces
- 800g desiree potatoes, peeled, cut into 3cm pieces
- 1 tablespoon Massel beef style stock powder
- 1 tablespoon worcestershire sauce

- 1/4 cup cornflour
- 1 cup frozen peas
- Crusty bread, to serve

Direction

- Place flour and chops in a large snap-lock bag. Seal. Shake to coat. Heat 1 tablespoon oil in a heavy-based saucepan over medium heat.
- Cook onion, celery and carrot, stirring, for 5 minutes or until onion has softened. Transfer to a bowl.
- Increase heat to high. Add 1 tablespoon oil. Cook half the chops for 2 minutes each side or until browned. Transfer to a plate.
- Repeat with remaining oil and chops. Layer 4 chops, half the potato and half the onion mixture in pan. Repeat layers with remaining chops, potato and onion mixture. Sprinkle over stock powder.
- Add Worcestershire sauce and 5 cups cold water. Bring to the boil, skimming off fat with a large metal spoon. Reduce heat to low. Cover. Cook for 2 hours, skimming off fat, or until lamb is cooked through and falling off the bone.
- Combine cornflour and 1/4 cup cold water in a jug. Increase heat to medium-high. Stir cornflour mixture and peas into stew. Cook, stirring occasionally, for 5 minutes or until gravy boils and thickens. Season with salt and pepper. Serve with crusty bread.

Nutrition Information

- Calories: 689.754 calories
- Saturated Fat: 6.9 grams saturated fat
- Total Fat: 24.2 grams fat
- Protein: 48 grams protein
- Cholesterol: 120 milligrams cholesterol
- Sodium: 1449 milligrams sodium
- Total Carbohydrate: 64.5 grams carbohydrates

62. Korma Lamb Cutlets With Biryani Rice

Serving: 4 | Prep: 15mins | Ready in: 55mins

Ingredients

- 1/3 cup (100g) korma curry paste
- 12 French-trimmed lamb cutlets
- 2 tablespoons sunflower oil
- 1 onion, finely chopped
- 2 garlic cloves, chopped
- 1 bay leaf
- 1 small cinnamon quill
- 5 cardamom pods, crushed
- 1 1/2 cups (300g) basmati rice
- 1 1/2 teaspoons ground turmeric
- 1/4 cup (20g) fried Asian shallots
- 1/4 cup (40g) raisins
- 1/2 red onion, thinly sliced
- 1/2 bunch mint, leaves picked
- Lemon wedges, to serve

Direction

- Brush curry paste over cutlets and set aside to marinate.
- Meanwhile, heat oil in a pan over medium heat. Cook onion, stirring, for 3-4 minutes until softened. Add garlic, bay, cinnamon and cardamom. Cook for a further 2 minutes or until fragrant. Add rice and stir to coat, then add 1L (4 cups) water. Bring to a simmer and cook for 20 minutes or until liquid is absorbed and rice is cooked. Transfer half the rice to a bowl. Keep warm. Return pan to medium heat. Add turmeric and 1 tbsp. water, and cook rice, stirring, for 2-3 minutes until coated. Remove from heat. Discard bay leaf and cinnamon quill.
- Preheat a chargrill pan to medium-high heat and cook cutlets, in batches, for 2 minutes each side for medium-rare or until cooked to your liking. Rest, loosely covered with foil, for 5 minutes.

- Combine both rice on a platter. Top with fried shallots, raisins, red onion and mint. Serve with cutlets and lemon wedges.

63. Lamb And Grilled Vegetable Salad

Serving: 4 | Prep: 15mins | Ready in: 33mins

Ingredients

- 2 corn cobs, cut into 3cm-thick rounds
- 1 bunch asparagus, woody ends trimmed
- 1 red capsicum, seeded and cut into thick strips
- 8-12 lamb cutlets, trimmed
- salt and cracked black pepper
- 1 teaspoon honey
- 2 teaspoons wholegrain mustard
- 1/4 cup olive oil
- 1 tablespoon lemon juice
- 1 bunch rocket, trimmed

Direction

- Heat a stovetop grill or barbecue over medium-high heat and spray with oil spray. Cook the corn, asparagus and capsicum in batches until tender and slightly charred. Remove and set aside.
- Spray the grill with extra oil and sprinkle the lamb cutlets with salt and cracked black pepper. Cook cutlets for 3 minutes each side or until cooked to your liking.
- Meanwhile, heat a small saucepan on low heat. Add the honey, mustard, oil and lemon juice and whisk until fully combined. Set aside to cool slightly.
- To serve, arrange the grilled corn, asparagus and capsicum on serving plates with the lamb and rocket. Drizzle with the dressing and serve.

Nutrition Information

- Calories: 483.736 calories
- Cholesterol: 121 milligrams cholesterol
- Sugar: 5 grams sugar
- Protein: 38 grams protein
- Sodium: 154.58 milligrams sodium
- Total Fat: 31 grams fat
- Saturated Fat: 9 grams saturated fat
- Total Carbohydrate: 11 grams carbohydrates

64. Lamb And Strawberry Quinoa Tabouli

Serving: 4 | Prep: 20mins | Ready in: 40mins

Ingredients

- 1 cup (200g) quinoa, rinsed, drained
- 1 garlic clove, crushed
- 1 lemon, juiced
- 2 tablespoons olive oil
- 8 Coles Australian Lamb Loin Chops
- 250g strawberries, coarsely chopped
- 1/2 cup finely chopped flat-leaf parsley
- 1/2 cup finely chopped mint
- 4 spring onions, thinly sliced
- 1 lemon, extra, zested, juiced

Direction

- Place the quinoa and 2 cups (500ml) water in a saucepan over medium heat. Bring to the boil. Reduce heat to low. Cook, covered, for 15 mins or until the quinoa is tender and liquid is absorbed. Remove from heat. Use a fork to separate the grains.
- Meanwhile, combine the garlic, lemon juice and half the oil in a shallow glass or ceramic dish. Add the lamb and toss to coat. Heat a barbecue grill or chargrill on medium-high. Cook the lamb, in batches, for 4 mins each side or until cooked to your liking. Set aside for 5 mins to rest.
- Combine the quinoa, strawberry, parsley, mint and spring onion in a large bowl. Season.

Combine the lemon zest, extra lemon juice and remaining oil in small jug. Season.
- Arrange the lamb and the quinoa mixture on a serving platter. Drizzle the lamb with the lemon juice mixture to serve.

65. Lamb And Warm Artichoke Salad

Serving: 4 | Prep: 15mins | Ready in: 25mins

Ingredients

- 2 cups (300g) frozen broad beans
- 1 lemon
- 1/4 cup (60ml) extra virgin olive oil
- 2 teaspoons sumac
- 12 lamb cutlets
- 8 marinated artichokes, cut into wedges
- 400g can cannelini beans, rinsed, drained
- 1 Spanish onion, thinly sliced
- 1/2 cup flat-leaf parsley leaves

Direction

- Cook the broad beans in a large saucepan of boiling water for 2 minutes or until tender. Drain well and remove and discard skins. Set aside.
- Use a zester to remove rind from lemon. (Alternatively, use a vegetable peeler to peel rind from lemon. Use a small, sharp knife to remove white pith from rind. Cut rind into very thin strips.) Juice the lemon. Combine the juice, rind and oil in a jug.
- Sprinkle sumac evenly over both sides of lamb. Heat a large frying pan over high heat. Add the lamb and cook for 2-3 minutes each side for medium or until cooked to your liking. Transfer to a plate, cover loosely with foil and set aside for 5 minutes to rest.
- Meanwhile, heat a large frying pan over high heat. Add the lemon mixture, artichoke, broad beans, cannellini beans and onion and cook, turning occasionally, for 2-3 minutes or until heated through. Remove from heat and add the parsley.
- Spoon the artichoke salad among serving dishes. Top with lamb cutlets and serve immediately.

Nutrition Information

- Calories: 543.008 calories
- Protein: 46 grams protein
- Cholesterol: 121 milligrams cholesterol
- Total Fat: 32 grams fat
- Saturated Fat: 9 grams saturated fat
- Total Carbohydrate: 12 grams carbohydrates
- Sugar: 4 grams sugar
- Sodium: 706.97 milligrams sodium

66. Lamb Bake With Crispy Potato Topping

Serving: 4 | Prep: 15mins | Ready in: 183mins

Ingredients

- 8 (1kg) small lamb forequarter or shoulder chops, trimmed
- 1/4 cup plain flour
- 1 tablespoon olive oil
- 1 large brown onion, roughly chopped
- 2 garlic cloves, crushed
- 3 medium carrots, peeled, cut into 3cm pieces
- 2 tablespoons tomato paste
- 2 1/2 cups Massel beef stock
- 2 dried bay leaves
- 1 cup frozen peas
- 3 cups (380g) frozen potato gems

Direction

- Preheat oven to 160°C/140°C fan-forced. Place lamb in a bowl. Add 1 tablespoon flour. Toss to coat. Heat oil in a frying pan over high heat. Cook lamb, in batches, for 3 minutes each side or until browned. Transfer lamb to a 28cm x

- 25.5cm, 10 cup-capacity ovenproof dish (with lid). Drain excess oil from pan.
- Add onion to pan over medium heat. Cook, stirring, for 3 minutes or until softened. Add garlic and carrot. Cook, stirring, for 2 minutes. Add tomato paste and remaining flour. Cook, stirring, for 1 minute. Stir in stock. Pour mixture over lamb. Add bay leaves. Season with pepper.
- Cover and bake for 1 hour 30 minutes. Remove lid. Bake for 30 minutes. Remove from oven. Skim excess fat. Remove and discard bay leaves.
- Increase temperature to 200°C/180°C fan-forced. Stir in peas. Sprinkle gems over top. Bake for 30 minutes or until gems are golden and crisp. Serve.

Nutrition Information

- Calories: 526.756 calories
- Total Carbohydrate: 36.5 grams carbohydrates
- Protein: 34.8 grams protein
- Sodium: 1500 milligrams sodium
- Total Fat: 24.9 grams fat
- Saturated Fat: 7.6 grams saturated fat
- Cholesterol: 99 milligrams cholesterol

67. Lamb Bake With Polenta

Serving: 4 | Prep: 10mins | Ready in: 50mins

Ingredients

- 4 cups Massel salt reduced chicken style liquid stock
- 1 1/4 cups instant polenta
- 8 lamb loin chops
- 2 x 400g cans chopped tomatoes
- 80g pitted kalamata olives
- 1 teaspoon dried oregano
- 200g fetta

Direction

- Place stock and 2 cups of cold water in a large saucepan. Bring to the boil over high heat. Gradually add polenta in a thin stream, whisking with a balloon whisk until well combined. Reduce heat to medium-low. Cook, stirring often, for 20 minutes or until grains are soft.
- Meanwhile, preheat oven to 200°C. Heat a large, non-stick frying pan over medium-high heat. Add lamb. Cook for 1 to 2 minutes on each side or until browned. Remove to a large baking dish.
- Spoon the tomatoes and olives over the lamb. Sprinkle with oregano. Season with pepper. Crumble the feta over the top. Bake for 15 minutes or until meat is cooked to your liking and sauce thickens.
- Spoon polenta onto serving plates. Top with lamb and spoon over sauce. Serve.

Nutrition Information

- Calories: 693.817 calories
- Total Fat: 37 grams fat
- Saturated Fat: 18 grams saturated fat
- Sugar: 11 grams sugar
- Protein: 46 grams protein
- Sodium: 1468 milligrams sodium
- Total Carbohydrate: 43 grams carbohydrates

68. Lamb Chops In Ratatouille

Serving: 4 | Prep: 15mins | Ready in: 60mins

Ingredients

- 1 tablespoon olive oil
- 8 lamb chops
- 1 large brown onion, chopped
- 2 garlic cloves, crushed
- 1 large zucchini, chopped
- 250g button mushrooms, halved
- 1/2 large eggplant, chopped
- 2 x 400g cans chopped tomatoes

- 2 tablespoons oregano leaves

Direction

- Heat oil in a large frying pan over medium-high heat. Cook lamb, in batches, for 2 to 3 minutes each side or until browned. Remove to a plate.
- Reduce heat to medium. Add onion and garlic to frying pan. Cook, stirring, for 2 minutes or until onion is soft. Add zucchini, mushrooms, eggplant and tomatoes. Return lamb to frying pan. Cover. Simmer gently for 30 minutes or until lamb is tender and sauce has thickened slightly. Stir through oregano. Season with salt and pepper. Serve.

Nutrition Information

- Calories: 456.49 calories
- Sugar: 11 grams sugar
- Protein: 35 grams protein
- Total Fat: 28 grams fat
- Saturated Fat: 11 grams saturated fat
- Total Carbohydrate: 14 grams carbohydrates
- Cholesterol: 85 milligrams cholesterol
- Sodium: 95.46 milligrams sodium

69. Lamb Chops With Greek Fattoush Salad

Serving: 4 | Prep: 15mins | Ready in: 30mins

Ingredients

- 1/4 cup (60ml) olive oil
- 2 garlic cloves, crushed
- 1/4 cup fresh oregano, finely chopped
- 1 lemon, zested and juiced
- 1 tablespoons red wine vinegar
- 8 (800g) Coles Australian lamb loin chops
- 1 large pita bread
- Olive oil, extra, to brush
- 350g mixed medley tomatoes, halved
- 1/2 red onion, thinly sliced
- 1/2 cup pitted kalamata olives
- 1 Lebanese cucumber, coarsely chopped
- 1/3 cup fresh oregano, extra
- 150g Greek feta, diced
- Lemon wedges, to serve

Direction

- Combine oil, garlic, oregano, lemon zest and juice, and red wine vinegar in a jug. Season. Place the chops in a glass or ceramic dish. Pour over 2/3 of the marinade. Set aside for 15 mins to marinate.
- Meanwhile, preheat oven to 180C. Brush pita bread with oil on both sides. Place on a lined baking tray. Bake for 5-8 mins or until crisp. Set aside to cool slightly.
- Place the tomato, onion, olives, cucumber, extra oregano and feta in a large bowl. Coarsely break the pita bread and add to bowl. Drizzle with remaining marinade, season and toss to coat.
- Heat a barbecue or chargrill on medium heat. Cook chops for 3 mins each side. Cover and set aside for 5 mins to rest. Serve chops with the salad and lemon wedges.

70. Lamb Chops With Greek Style Salad

Serving: 4 | Prep: 20mins | Ready in: 40mins

Ingredients

- 800g red potatoes, peeled
- 250g punnet cherry tomatoes, halved
- 1/3 cup pitted kalamata olives
- 2 tablespoons balsamic dressing
- 100g fetta cheese, crumbled
- Olive oil, to shallow fry
- 8 lamb loin chops
- 1 lebanese cucumber
- 1 cos lettuce, outer leaves removed, torn

Direction

- Cut the potatoes into 1.5-2cm cubes. Heat about 5mm oil in a large heavy based frying pan. Cook the potatoes for 15-20 mins turning often until crisp and golden. Drain on kitchen paper.
- Meanwhile, cook chops in another lightly oiled large frying pan for 4 mins each side.
- To make Greek-style salad cut cucumber into quarters lengthways then into pieces. Combine with tomatoes, lettuce, olives and dressing. Toss to combine then add feta.
- Serve chops with the potatoes and salad.

71. Lamb Chops With An Italianate Stuffing

Serving: 4 | Prep: 25mins | Ready in: 45mins

Ingredients

- 12 x 15cm-long sprigs rosemary
- 250g punnet cherry tomatoes, halved
- 160g piece crustless Italian-style bread, cut into 5mm cubes
- 120g pecorino or parmesan, finely grated
- 1/3 cup (65g) currants, soaked in warm water for 20 minutes, drained
- 1/3 cup (50g) pine nuts, lightly toasted, coarsely chopped
- 2 (55g each) eggs
- 2 cloves garlic, 1 finely chopped, 1 thinly sliced
- 8 (150g each) lamb loin chops
- 2 teaspoons olive oil
- 1/2 cup (125ml) balsamic vinegar
- 2 teaspoons caster sugar
- Baby rocket leaves, to serve

Direction

- Strip all but 2cm of rosemary leaves from sprigs, then finely chop 1 teaspoon leaves and reserve 2 teaspoons whole leaves. Thread tomato halves on to rosemary sprigs.
- Combine bread, cheese, currants, pine nuts, eggs, and chopped rosemary and garlic. Season with salt and pepper. Press 1/8 stuffing next to meat on each chop, then wrap tail around and secure with string.
- Preheat oven to 180°C. Heat oil in a frying pan over medium-high heat. Cook chops for 3 minutes each side and a further 2 minutes on fat side. Place on an oven tray and roast for 10 minutes or until cooked.
- Heat same frying pan over medium heat. Cook tomato skewers, sliced garlic and rosemary leaves, in 2 batches, for 15 seconds each side. Remove skewers. Add vinegar and sugar and simmer until reduced by 1/2. Serve chops, drizzled with vinegar, with tomato skewers and rocket.

Nutrition Information

- Calories: 1215.793 calories
- Protein: 91 grams protein
- Total Fat: 79 grams fat
- Saturated Fat: 32 grams saturated fat
- Total Carbohydrate: 34 grams carbohydrates
- Sugar: 16 grams sugar
- Cholesterol: 338 milligrams cholesterol
- Sodium: 701.75 milligrams sodium

72. Lamb Chops With Harissa Yoghurt

Serving: 4 | Prep: 15mins | Ready in: 25mins

Ingredients

- 500g sweet potato, washed
- 2 tablespoons olive oil
- 4 (200g each) lamb forequarter chops
- 3/4 cup Coles Simply Less light Greek-style yoghurt
- 2 teaspoons harissa paste (see note)
- 2 tablespoons chopped fresh coriander leaves
- 2 witlof, leaves separated

- 1 cup fresh flat-leaf parsley leaves
- 1/2 cup fresh coriander leaves
- 1 tablespoon lemon juice
- Lemon wedges, to serve

Direction

- Using a fork, pierce sweet potato all over. Place on a microwave-safe plate. Microwave on HIGH (100%) for 4 minutes or until tender. Quarter sweet potato lengthways. Brush with half the oil.
- Heat a greased barbecue plate or chargrill on medium-high. Cook lamb for 3 to 4 minutes each side for medium or until cooked to your liking. Cook sweet potato for 2 to 3 minutes each side or until crisp.
- Place yoghurt, harissa paste and chopped coriander in a small bowl. Stir to combine.
- Combine witlof, parsley leaves and coriander leaves in a medium bowl. Drizzle with lemon juice and remaining oil. Toss gently to combine. Drizzle sweet potato with harissa yoghurt. Serve lamb chops with sweet potato, salad and lemon wedges.

Nutrition Information

- Calories: 649.841 calories
- Total Fat: 46 grams fat
- Saturated Fat: 13 grams saturated fat
- Total Carbohydrate: 24 grams carbohydrates
- Sugar: 13 grams sugar
- Cholesterol: 103 milligrams cholesterol
- Protein: 34 grams protein
- Sodium: 225.58 milligrams sodium

73. Lamb Chops With Lemony Asparagus Recipe

Serving: 4 | Prep: 10mins | Ready in: 30mins

Ingredients

- ½ cup (140g) Greek-style yoghurt
- 6 tbs extra virgin olive oil, divided
- 1 garlic clove, finely chopped
- 1 tsp ground cumin
- 1 tsp ground coriander
- 1/2 tsp ground turmeric
- 4 Coles Australian Lamb Forequarter Chops (about 200g each)
- 2 lemons, rind finely grated, juiced
- 1 tbs finely chopped flat-leaf parsley
- 2 bunches asparagus, woody ends trimmed
- 8 spring onions, trimmed
- 3 radishes, very thinly sliced
- 1/2 cup flat-leaf parsley sprigs
- Lemon wedges, to serve

Direction

- In a medium bowl, whisk the yoghurt and 1 tbsp. of the oil with garlic, cumin, coriander, turmeric, 1 tsp. sea salt flakes and ½ tsp. freshly ground black pepper. Add the lamb and turn to coat. Set aside for 30 mins to marinate.
- Prepare a barbecue for medium-high heat. In a medium bowl, whisk the lemon rind, ⅓ cup (80ml) lemon juice, ⅓ cup (80ml) oil, chopped parsley, ¾ tsp. salt and ¼ tsp. pepper.
- Remove the lamb from the marinade and wipe off the excess. Barbecue the lamb for 5-6 mins each side or until browned on both sides and internal temperature is 54°C for medium-rare doneness. Transfer the lamb to a serving platter. Spoon half the lemon juice mixture over the lamb and set aside for 5 mins to rest.
- While the lamb is resting, combine asparagus, spring onions and remaining 1 tbsp. of oil in a bowl. Season with salt and pepper. Barbecue the asparagus mixture, turning occasionally, for 4 mins or until the asparagus and spring onions are charred all over and asparagus is just tender.
- Transfer the asparagus mixture to the serving platter with the lamb. Drizzle with remaining dressing. Top with the radish and parsley sprigs. Serve with the lemon wedges.

Nutrition Information

- Calories: 533.687 calories
- Saturated Fat: 14 grams saturated fat
- Sodium: 849 milligrams sodium
- Total Fat: 42 grams fat
- Total Carbohydrate: 6 grams carbohydrates
- Sugar: 5 grams sugar
- Protein: 32 grams protein

74. Lamb Chops With Oregano And Lemon

Serving: 4 | Prep: 15mins | Ready in: 25mins

Ingredients

- 1 teaspoon finely grated lemon rind
- 2 tablespoons lemon juice
- 1/4 cup olive oil
- 1 tablespoon finely chopped fresh oregano leaves
- 2 garlic cloves, crushed
- 8 x 100g lamb chump chops
- 1 red capsicum, thickly sliced
- 1 yellow capsicum, thickly sliced
- 100g baby rocket
- 75g drained marinated artichoke quarters
- 75g feta, crumbled

Direction

- Combine lemon rind and half the lemon juice, oil, oregano and garlic in a large shallow dish. Add lamb. Turn to coat in mixture. Cover. Refrigerate for 1 hour, if time permits.
- Heat a barbecue chargrill or chargrill pan on medium-high heat. Toss capsicums in 2 teaspoons remaining oil. Cook capsicums, turning, for 6 minutes or until lightly charred and tender. Transfer to a large bowl. Add lamb to chargrill. Cook for 3 to 4 minutes each side for medium or until cooked to your liking.
- Add rocket, artichokes and feta to capsicum. Place remaining lemon juice, oil, oregano and garlic in a small bowl. Whisk until combined. Season with salt and pepper. Add dressing to salad. Toss gently to combine. Serve salad with lamb chops.

Nutrition Information

- Calories: 560.933 calories
- Cholesterol: 142 milligrams cholesterol
- Sodium: 387.52 milligrams sodium
- Total Carbohydrate: 3 grams carbohydrates
- Sugar: 3 grams sugar
- Total Fat: 40 grams fat
- Saturated Fat: 13 grams saturated fat
- Protein: 47 grams protein

75. Lamb Chops With Polenta

Serving: 4 | Prep: 10mins | Ready in: 25mins

Ingredients

- 4 lamb forequarter chops
- 2 tablespoons chopped fresh chives
- 1 tablespoon chopped fresh rosemary leaves
- 2 tablespoons olive oil
- 1 small brown onion, finely chopped
- 1 x 400g can diced tomatoes
- 1/2 teaspoon caster sugar
- 500ml (2 cups) Massel chicken style liquid stock
- 375ml (1 1/2 cups) water
- 170g (1 cup) instant polenta (cornmeal)
- 60g butter
- Chopped fresh continental parsley, to serve

Direction

- Combine lamb, chives, rosemary and 1 tablespoon of oil in a bowl. Season with pepper. Cover and place in the fridge.

- Heat remaining oil in a saucepan over medium heat. Add the onion and cook, stirring, for 3 minutes or until soft. Add tomato and sugar and bring to a simmer. Cook for 8 minutes or until the sauce thickens. Season with salt and pepper.
- Meanwhile, heat a frying pan over medium-high heat. Add lamb and cook for 3-5 minutes each side for medium or until cooked to your liking. Transfer to a plate and cover with foil to keep warm.
- Bring stock and water to the boil in a saucepan over high heat. Reduce heat to medium. Gradually add the polenta in a thin, steady stream, stirring until combined. Cook, stirring, for 4 minutes. Stir in the butter. Season with pepper.
- Divide the polenta and lamb among serving plates. Drizzle over the tomato sauce. Sprinkle with parsley to serve.

Nutrition Information

- Calories: 717.478 calories
- Cholesterol: 118 milligrams cholesterol
- Sodium: 809.69 milligrams sodium
- Saturated Fat: 17 grams saturated fat
- Total Carbohydrate: 35 grams carbohydrates
- Sugar: 5 grams sugar
- Protein: 30 grams protein
- Total Fat: 51 grams fat

76. Lamb Chops With Polenta, Sun Dried Tomatoes And Pesto

Serving: 4 | Prep: 5mins | Ready in: 15mins

Ingredients

- 8 lamb chops, tails trimmed
- 30g unsalted butter
- 2/3 cup sun-dried tomatoes
- 1/2 cup store-bought pesto
- 2 cups hot Massel chicken style liquid stock
- 1 1/2 cups instant polenta

Direction

- Heat a little oil in a non-stick frying pan over high heat. Sprinkle lamb chop with salt and pepper. Add to pan and cook in batches for 2-3 minutes each side or until cooked to your liking. Remove, cover and keep warm.
- Meanwhile, heat stock in a saucepan over medium heat, until simmering. Add polenta and stir until soft and thick. Stir in butter and remove from heat.
- Divide polenta between four serving bowls. Top each with lamb, scatter over sun-dried tomatoes and add a spoonful of pesto.

Nutrition Information

- Calories: 721.063 calories
- Sugar: 9 grams sugar
- Cholesterol: 104 milligrams cholesterol
- Sodium: 981.91 milligrams sodium
- Total Fat: 43 grams fat
- Saturated Fat: 16 grams saturated fat
- Total Carbohydrate: 44 grams carbohydrates
- Protein: 38 grams protein

77. Lamb Chops With Potato And Pea Salad

Serving: 4 | Prep: 15mins | Ready in: 30mins

Ingredients

- 6 chat potatoes, halved
- 1 bunch asparagus, trimmed, cut into 4cm lengths
- 100g sugar snap peas, trimmed
- 2 1/2 tablespoons olive oil
- 4 (180g each) lamb forequarter chops, trimmed
- 1/4 cup pepitas (pumpkin seeds), toasted
- 1 tablespoon white wine vinegar

Direction

- Place potato in a saucepan. Cover with cold water. Bring to the boil over high heat. Cook for 10 minutes or until tender. Add asparagus and peas to pan for last 3 minutes of cooking. Drain. Rinse under cold water. Drain. Return to pan.
- Meanwhile, heat 2 teaspoons oil in a large frying pan over medium-high heat. Add lamb. Cook for 3 to 4 minutes each side for medium or until cooked to your liking.
- Add pepitas, vinegar and remaining oil to potato mixture. Toss to combine. Serve lamb with potato mixture.

Nutrition Information

- Calories: 613.752 calories
- Saturated Fat: 11 grams saturated fat
- Total Carbohydrate: 19 grams carbohydrates
- Cholesterol: 88 milligrams cholesterol
- Sodium: 92.35 milligrams sodium
- Total Fat: 45 grams fat
- Sugar: 2 grams sugar
- Protein: 32 grams protein

78. Lamb Chops With Roast Vegetables

Serving: 4 | Prep: 5mins | Ready in: 25mins

Ingredients

- 250g punnet cherry tomatoes, halved
- 2 zucchini, halved lengthways, cut into 3cm lengths
- 2 baby eggplant, halved lengthways
- 2 tablespoons olive oil
- 2 teaspoons rosemary, chopped
- 8 lamb chops
- 100g baby spinach leaves

Direction

- Preheat oven to 220°C. Line a roasting pan with baking paper.
- Combine vegetables, 1 1/2 tablespoons of oil, rosemary, and salt and pepper. Toss to combine. Place into a large roasting pan. Roast for 15 to 20 minutes, or until vegetables are golden and tender.
- Heat remaining 2 teaspoons of oil in a frying pan over medium-high heat. Cook lamb for 3 minutes each side for medium.
- Serve lamb with vegetables and spinach.

Nutrition Information

- Calories: 428.049 calories
- Total Fat: 32 grams fat
- Total Carbohydrate: 3 grams carbohydrates
- Sugar: 3 grams sugar
- Cholesterol: 85 milligrams cholesterol
- Saturated Fat: 12 grams saturated fat
- Protein: 31 grams protein
- Sodium: 81.98 milligrams sodium

79. Lamb Chops With Roasted Ratatouille

Serving: 4 | Prep: 20mins | Ready in: 55mins

Ingredients

- 1 red onion, halved, cut into wedges
- 1 red capsicum, roughly chopped
- 1 zucchini, thickly sliced
- 2 tomatoes, roughly chopped
- 1 small eggplant, trimmed, roughly chopped
- 2 tablespoons extra virgin olive oil
- 2 garlic cloves, sliced
- 2 large sprigs fresh basil, plus extra leaves to serve
- 8 lamb loin chops
- 1 tablespoon balsamic vinegar
- 1/3 cup pitted kalamata olives
- Crusty bread, to serve

Direction

- Preheat oven to 200C/180C fan-forced. Line a large baking tray with sides with baking paper.
- Arrange onion, capsicum, zucchini, tomato and eggplant in separate rows on prepared tray, in a single layer. Drizzle with 1/2 the oil. Season with salt and pepper. Roast for 20 minutes.
- Sprinkle garlic over vegetables and top with basil sprigs. Place lamb on vegetables. Drizzle lamb with vinegar and remaining oil. Season with salt and pepper. Roast for a further 15 minutes, adding olives to the vegetables in the last 5 minutes of cooking. Serve with bread, sprinkled with extra basil leaves.

Nutrition Information

- Calories: 699.553 calories
- Sodium: 655 milligrams sodium
- Total Carbohydrate: 34.5 grams carbohydrates
- Protein: 39 grams protein
- Cholesterol: 98 milligrams cholesterol
- Total Fat: 44 grams fat
- Saturated Fat: 16 grams saturated fat

80. Lamb Chops With Sundried Tomato And Basil Butter

Serving: 4 | Prep: 20mins | Ready in: 30mins

Ingredients

- 8 (1kg) lamb chump chops
- 600g kipfler potatoes, washed
- 2 tablespoons olive oil
- Small basil leaves, to serve
- Mixed salad leaves, to serve
- 50g butter, softened
- 1/4 cup drained sundried tomatoes
- 1 garlic clove, crushed
- 2 tablespoons chopped fresh basil leaves

Direction

- Make Sundried tomato and basil butter: Place butter, tomato, garlic and basil in a food processor. Process until combined. Spoon mixture along the center of a 25cm piece of baking paper. Roll paper to enclose butter and form a log shape. Wrap in plastic wrap. Refrigerate for 2 hours or until required.
- Heat a barbecue plate or chargrill on medium-high heat. Cook lamb chops for 3 to 4 minutes each side for medium or until cooked to your liking.
- Meanwhile, pierce potatoes all over with a fork. Place on a large plate. Microwave, on High (100%) for 4 minutes or until just tender. Thickly slice potatoes diagonally. Place in a medium bowl. Add oil. Toss to coat. Season with salt and pepper. Cook potato on barbecue plate or chargrill for 1 to 2 minutes each side or until golden and crisp.
- Unwrap butter log. Thickly slice. Serve lamb chops topped with butter slices, grilled potatoes, basil and salad leaves.

Nutrition Information

- Calories: 709.352 calories
- Total Fat: 51.4 grams fat
- Saturated Fat: 21.1 grams saturated fat
- Total Carbohydrate: 23.1 grams carbohydrates
- Protein: 39.8 grams protein
- Cholesterol: 144 milligrams cholesterol
- Sodium: 247 milligrams sodium

81. Lamb Chops With White Bean Puree And Fresh Herb Salad

Serving: 4 | Prep: 15mins | Ready in: 20mins

Ingredients

- 420g can cannellini beans
- 2 garlic cloves, crushed

- 1/4 teaspoon ground cumin
- 1/3 cup (80ml) fresh lemon juice
- 4 lamb forequarter chops
- Sea salt freshly ground black pepper
- 2 cups coriander sprigs
- 1 cup small mint leaves
- 2 tablespoons finely chopped red onion
- 1/3 cup roasted yellow pepper strips, finely chopped
- 2 tablespoons extra virgin olive oil

Direction

- Blend or process beans, garlic, cumin and half the lemon juice until smooth. Season to taste.
- Spray chops lightly with oil and season. Cook chops on a heated grill plate for 2 minutes on each side, or until cooked to your liking. Remove from heat, cover with foil and rest for 5 minutes.
- Meanwhile, combine coriander, mint, onion, peppers, oil and remaining lemon juice in a medium bowl. Serve chops topped with white bean puree and fresh herb salad.

Nutrition Information

- Calories: 572.405 calories
- Protein: 33 grams protein
- Sodium: 341.11 milligrams sodium
- Saturated Fat: 9 grams saturated fat
- Total Carbohydrate: 24 grams carbohydrates
- Total Fat: 38 grams fat
- Sugar: 3 grams sugar
- Cholesterol: 84 milligrams cholesterol

82. Lamb Cutlets And Rosemary Gravy

Serving: 4 | Prep: 50mins | Ready in: 75mins

Ingredients

- 3/4 cup plain flour
- 2 eggs, lightly beaten
- 3 cups fresh white breadcrumbs
- 1/4 cup sesame seeds
- 12 lamb cutlets, trimmed
- 40g butter
- 2 tablespoons olive oil
- 29g packet Gravox Lamb with Rosemary Flavoured Gravy Mix
- 1 cup cold water
- Oven-baked fries, to serve
- Salad, to serve

Direction

- Preheat oven to 180°C. Place flour onto a plate and eggs into a dish. Combine breadcrumbs and sesame seeds. Dip cutlets into flour then egg. Coat with breadcrumb mixture, pressing on with your fingers. Refrigerate for 30 minutes.
- Heat half the butter and half the oil in a frying pan over medium heat. Cook cutlets, 6 at a time, for 4 minutes each side, adding more butter and oil as needed. Keep warm in oven.
- Combine gravy mix and water in a saucepan over medium heat. Cook, stirring, for 4 minutes or until gravy comes to the boil. Reduce heat to low. Simmer for 5 minutes. Serve cutlets and gravy with fries and salad.

Nutrition Information

- Calories: 803.04 calories
- Saturated Fat: 15 grams saturated fat
- Sugar: 2 grams sugar
- Protein: 49 grams protein
- Cholesterol: 252 milligrams cholesterol
- Total Fat: 43 grams fat
- Total Carbohydrate: 53 grams carbohydrates
- Sodium: 1111.42 milligrams sodium

83. Lamb Cutlets With Bean Salad

Serving: 4 | Prep: 5mins | Ready in: 10mins

Ingredients

- 400g can four bean mix, rinsed, drained
- 250g can cherry tomatoes, quartered
- 150g rocket
- 1/4 cup balsamic dressing
- 12 lamb cutlets
- 1 small red onion, thinly sliced

Direction

- Preheat a chargrill or barbecue on high. Cook lamb for 2-3 mins each side, until cooked to your liking.
- Meanwhile, combine remaining ingredients in a salad bowl. Serve lamb with bean salad.
- Heat a barbecue or chargrill to high and cook lamb, in batches if necessary, 2-3 minutes each side. Cook lemon slices for 1 minute. Toss salad with dressing and serve with lamb and lemon.

Nutrition Information

- Calories: 877.847 calories
- Total Fat: 68 grams fat
- Saturated Fat: 26 grams saturated fat
- Sugar: 7 grams sugar
- Sodium: 1306.93 milligrams sodium
- Total Carbohydrate: 9 grams carbohydrates
- Protein: 57 grams protein

84. Lamb Cutlets With Bean, Strawberry And Feta Salad

Serving: 4 | Prep: 65mins | Ready in: 75mins

Ingredients

- 12 french-trimmed lamb cutlets
- 1/2 cup (125ml) olive oil
- 2 lemons, very thinly sliced
- 1 bunch mint, leaves picked
- 2 tablespoons raspberry* or red wine vinegar
- 2 teaspoons caster sugar
- 1 tablespoon Dijon mustard
- 500g French or thin green beans, blanched
- 400g small strawberries, sliced
- 400g feta, crumbled

Direction

- Place lamb in a shallow dish and drizzle with 100ml oil. Add the lemon slices, half the mint, and season. Toss to coat, cover and refrigerate for 1 hour.
- Whisk remaining oil, vinegar, sugar, mustard, salt and pepper. Toss together beans, berries, feta and remaining mint.

85. Lamb Cutlets With Braised Cannellini Beans Rosemary

Serving: 4 | Prep: 10mins | Ready in: 40mins

Ingredients

- Olive oil spray
- 1 brown onion, finely chopped
- 2 celery sticks, trimmed, finely chopped
- 2 garlic cloves, thinly sliced
- 2 teaspoons fresh rosemary leaves
- 2 x 250g punnets cherry tomatoes, halved
- 2 x 400g cans cannellini beans, rinsed, drained
- 2 teaspoons brown sugar
- 8 lamb cutlets, French trimmed
- 250g green beans, topped

Direction

- Preheat oven to 180°C. Heat a large flameproof ovenproof dish over medium heat. Spray with olive oil spray to lightly grease. Add the onion and celery and cook, stirring occasionally, for 5 minutes or until the onion softens. Add the garlic and rosemary, and cook, stirring, for 1 minute or until aromatic.

- Stir in the tomato, cannellini beans and sugar. Cover. Bake for 20 minutes or until the tomato softens. Season with pepper.
- Heat a non-stick frying pan over high heat. Spray with olive oil spray to lightly grease. Add the lamb. Cook for 2 minutes each side for medium or until cooked to your liking. Transfer to a plate and cover with foil. Set aside for 2 minutes to rest.
- Meanwhile, cook the green beans in a steamer over a saucepan of boiling water (make sure the steamer doesn't touch the water), covered, for 3 minutes or until bright green and tender crisp.
- Divide the cannellini bean mixture and green beans among serving plates. Top with lamb cutlets to serve.

Nutrition Information

- Calories: 386.941 calories
- Protein: 35 grams protein
- Cholesterol: 80 milligrams cholesterol
- Sodium: 410.51 milligrams sodium
- Total Fat: 12 grams fat
- Saturated Fat: 4 grams saturated fat
- Sugar: 7 grams sugar
- Total Carbohydrate: 32 grams carbohydrates

86. Lamb Cutlets With Broad Bean Mash

Serving: 4 | Prep: 45mins | Ready in: 51mins

Ingredients

- 2 tablespoons olive oil
- 1/4 cup thick mint sauce
- 8 lamb cutlets, trimmed
- 500g frozen broad beans
- 2 tablespoons sour cream
- potato wedges, to serve

Direction

- Combine oil and sauce in a large glass or ceramic dish. Add cutlets. Turn to coat. Refrigerate for 30 minutes if time permits.
- Preheat a barbecue plate or chargrill over high heat. Reduce heat to medium. Cook lamb, basting with marinade, for 3 minutes each side for medium or until cooked to your liking. Transfer to a plate. Cover with foil. Set aside for 5 minutes to rest.
- Meanwhile, place broad beans in a heatproof, microwave-safe bowl. Add 1/4 cup cold water. Cover with plastic wrap. Microwave on high (100%) for 4 to 5 minutes or until tender. Drain. Rinse under cold water. Remove and discard skins. Return beans to bowl. Cover. Microwave on high (100%) for 1 minute. Roughly mash. Add sour cream. Season with salt and pepper. Stir to combine.
- Serve lamb with mash and wedges.

Nutrition Information

- Calories: 344.16 calories
- Cholesterol: 73 milligrams cholesterol
- Total Fat: 20.4 grams fat
- Saturated Fat: 7.6 grams saturated fat
- Total Carbohydrate: 12.5 grams carbohydrates
- Protein: 25.9 grams protein
- Sodium: 154 milligrams sodium

87. Lamb Cutlets With Burghul And Eggplant Pilaf

Serving: 4 | Prep: 5mins | Ready in: 25mins

Ingredients

- 2 tablespoons extra virgin olive oil
- 1 red onion, thinly sliced
- 2 garlic cloves, thinly sliced
- 1 eggplant, cut into 2cm cubes
- 2 teaspoons chopped fresh rosemary
- 1 1/2 cups (240g) burghul (see note) (cracked wheat)

- 2 cups (500ml) chicken consomme (see note) or Massel chicken style liquid stock
- 12 French-trimmed lamb cutlets
- Olive oil spray
- 1/2 cup (85g) raisins
- 1/4 cup chopped mint leaves, plus small whole leaves to garnish

Direction

- Heat oil in a deep fry pan over medium heat. Add onion and garlic and gently cook, stirring, for 2-3 minutes until soft. Add eggplant and rosemary and cook for a further 5 minutes or until lightly browned. Stir in burghul, then pour in consommé. Bring to the boil, then cover and simmer gently for 10 minutes until stock has absorbed and burghul has softened.
- Meanwhile, heat a chargrill or large non-stick fry pan over high heat. Season lamb, lightly spray with oil, and then cook for 3-4 minutes each side until lamb is cooked but still pink in the centre. Leave lamb to rest while you stir raisins and mint into the burghul and season to taste. Serve lamb on pilaf, garnished with mint leaves.

Nutrition Information

- Calories: 611.601 calories
- Total Carbohydrate: 53.7 grams carbohydrates
- Total Fat: 23.1 grams fat
- Saturated Fat: 6.4 grams saturated fat
- Protein: 39.3 grams protein
- Cholesterol: 90 milligrams cholesterol
- Sodium: 795 milligrams sodium

88. Lamb Cutlets With Carrot And Broad Bean Salad Recipe

Serving: 4 | Prep: 10mins | Ready in: 30mins

Ingredients

- 2 bunches Dutch carrots*, peeled, ends trimmed
- 500g pkt frozen broad beans
- 12 Coles Australian Lamb Cutlets
- 1 bunch mint, leaves picked
- 200g Coles Beetroot Dip

Direction

- Preheat oven to 200°C. Line a baking tray with baking paper. Arrange carrots over lined tray. Spray with olive oil spray. Season. Roast, turning occasionally, for 15-20 mins or until tender.
- Meanwhile, cook the broad beans in a saucepan of boiling water for 2 mins or until heated through. Refresh under cold water. Drain. Peel. Place in a bowl.
- Heat a chargrill on high. Season the lamb and cook for 2-3 mins each side for medium or until cooked to your liking. Set aside for 5 mins to rest.
- Add carrots and mint to the broad beans in the bowl. Toss to combine. Arrange the lamb and salad on serving plates. Season. Serve with beetroot dip.

89. Lamb Cutlets With Char Grilled Vegetable Couscous

Serving: 4 | Prep: 10mins | Ready in: 20mins

Ingredients

- 8 lamb cutlets, trimmed
- 1 tablespoons olive oil
- 2 teaspoons ground coriander
- 2 teaspoons ground cumin
- 8 button mushrooms, quartered
- 2 zucchini, halved, thinly sliced
- 2 onions, cut into eighths
- 1 red capsicum, seeded, thickly sliced
- 1 cup couscous
- 1 cup hot Campbell's Real Stock Vegetable
- 3 green onion, sliced

Direction

- Brush cutlets with half the oil and toss in combined spices. Arrange on a tray and chill until required. Preheat char-grill on high.
- Place couscous in a bowl and pour stock over. Cover for 5 minutes until stock is absorbed. Fluff with a fork. Season to taste and mix onion through.
- Brush vegetables with remaining oil and char-grill 1-2 minutes each side. Toss through couscous. Char-grill lamb for 2-3 minutes each side and serve with couscous.

90. Lamb Cutlets With Chickpea Puree And Grilled Zucchini Salad

Serving: 0 | Prep: 15mins | Ready in: 30mins

Ingredients

- 2 x 400g cans chickpeas, rinsed, drained
- 2 garlic cloves, crushed
- 80ml (1/3 cup) fresh lemon juice
- 80ml (1/3 cup) extra virgin olive oil
- 3 zucchini, peeled into ribbons
- 12 French-trimmed lamb cutlets
- 1 cup fresh mint leaves
- 1 cup fresh parsley leaves
- 1 cup fresh basil leaves
- 2 tablespoons capers, rinsed, drained
- 4 anchovy fillets, chopped
- 80ml (1/3 cup) extra virgin olive oil

Direction

- To make the salsa verde, process the mint, parsley, basil, capers and anchovies in a food processor until finely chopped. With the motor running, slowly add the oil until smooth and combined. Season well. Add a little water to thin the consistency, if needed. Transfer to a bowl. Set aside.
- Use paper towel to wipe the bowl of the food processor clean. Add the chickpeas, garlic, lemon juice and 1/4 cup oil. Process until the mixture is almost smooth.
- Meanwhile, preheat a chargrill pan or barbecue grill on medium. Combine the zucchini ribbons and remaining oil in a bowl. Season. Cook zucchini, turning, for 3 minutes or until charred and tender. Transfer to a plate.
- Season the lamb cutlets. Add to the pan or grill and cook for 4-5 minutes each side for medium or until cooked to your liking. Transfer to a plate and set aside for 3 minutes to rest.
- Season the lamb cutlets. Add to the pan or grill and cook for 4-5 minutes each side for medium or until cooked to your liking. Transfer to a plate and set aside for 3 minutes to rest.

91. Lamb Cutlets With Chilli Olive Salsa

Serving: 4 | Prep: 15mins | Ready in: 25mins

Ingredients

- 12 lamb cutlets, French trimmed
- 1 tablespoon chopped fresh lemon thyme
- 2 garlic cloves, crushed
- 1 tablespoon olive oil
- 1 x 80g pkt baby rocket leaves
- Bought babaghanoush, to serve
- Crusty bread, to serve
- 160g (1 cup) pimiento-stuffed green olives, chopped
- 1 long fresh green chilli, deseeded, chopped
- 1 long fresh red chilli, deseeded, chopped
- 1 long fresh yellow chilli, deseeded, chopped
- 2 teaspoons olive oil
- 2 teaspoons fresh lemon juice

Direction

- To make the salsa, place the olives, combined chilli, oil and lemon juice in a bowl and season with salt and pepper.
- Meanwhile, combine the lamb, thyme, garlic and oil in a glass or ceramic dish. Cover with plastic wrap and set aside for 15 minutes to marinate.
- Preheat a barbecue or chargrill on high. Season the lamb with salt and pepper. Cook on grill for 2-3 minutes each side for medium or until cooked to your liking. Transfer to a plate. Cover with foil and set aside for 5 minutes to rest.
- Divide the rocket among serving plates. Top with lamb and spoon over salsa. Serve with baba ghanoush and bread.

Nutrition Information

- Calories: 385.985 calories
- Sugar: 1 grams sugar
- Saturated Fat: 8 grams saturated fat
- Protein: 35 grams protein
- Cholesterol: 121 milligrams cholesterol
- Sodium: 955.6 milligrams sodium
- Total Fat: 26 grams fat
- Total Carbohydrate: 2 grams carbohydrates

92. Lamb Cutlets With Eggplant Basil Fry Up And Quick Chilli Pickle

Serving: 4 | Prep: 15mins | Ready in: 35mins

Ingredients

- 60g (1/4 cup) coconut oil
- 1 red onion, cut into thin wedges
- 4cm piece ginger, peeled, cut into matchsticks
- 2 garlic cloves, thinly sliced
- 400g eggplant, halved, sliced diagonally
- 1 tablespoon water
- 300g green beans, trimmed, halved diagonally
- 1 cup fresh basil leaves, firmly packed
- 12 French-trimmed lamb cutlets
- Small basil leaves, extra, to serve
- 2 tablespoons mirin seasoning
- 2 tablespoons rice wine vinegar
- 1 1/2 teaspoons caster sugar
- 1/2 teaspoon sea salt
- 1 long fresh red chilli, thinly sliced diagonally
- 1 star anise

Direction

- For the pickle, combine all the ingredients in a microwave-safe bowl. Microwave on high for 1 minute. Stir to dissolve. Set aside.
- Heat 2 1/2 tbsp. coconut oil in a large non-stick frying pan over high heat. Add the onion. Cook, stirring, for 1 minute or until just soft. Stir in the ginger and garlic for 1 minute or until aromatic. Add the eggplant. Cook, stirring, for 3 minutes. Add the water and half the chilli pickle. Cook, stirring, for 3 minutes or until eggplant is tender. Stir in the beans for 2-3 minutes or until tender crisp. Remove from heat. Stir through the basil. Season. Transfer to a bowl. Keep warm.
- Heat remaining oil in pan over medium-high heat. Season lamb. Cook, turning, for 4 minutes for medium or until cooked to your liking. Arrange eggplant mixture and lamb cutlets on a serving platter. Drizzle over a little of the remaining chilli pickle and top with extra basil leaves. Serve with the remaining pickle.

Nutrition Information

- Calories: 820.248 calories
- Sugar: 9.9 grams sugar
- Protein: 88.3 grams protein
- Sodium: 619 milligrams sodium
- Total Fat: 38.1 grams fat
- Saturated Fat: 21.1 grams saturated fat
- Total Carbohydrate: 29.6 grams carbohydrates
- Cholesterol: 270 milligrams cholesterol

93. Lamb Cutlets With Feta And Prosciutto

Serving: 8 | Prep: 10mins | Ready in: 16mins

Ingredients

- 16 lamb cutlets, french-trimmed
- 200g feta cheese, cut into 16 slices
- 16 small rosemary sprigs
- 300g fresh prosciutto, from the deli
- 2 tablespoons honey

Direction

- Using your hand, press cutlets to flatten meat slightly. Top each cutlet with a slice of feta and a sprig of rosemary. Wrap a slice of prosciutto around feta, to enclose.
- Preheat barbecue plate or chargrill on medium. Cook cutlets for 2-3 mins each side, for medium-rare, or until cooked to your liking.
- Transfer to a platter and drizzle over honey.

94. Lamb Cutlets With Green Mash Mint Sauce

Serving: 4 | Prep: 10mins | Ready in: 30mins

Ingredients

- 700g Sebago potatoes, peeled, coarsely chopped
- 230g (1 1/2 cups) frozen baby peas
- 1 green shallot, thinly sliced
- 1 1/2 tablespoons reduced-fat milk, warmed
- 50g baby spinach leaves
- 250g cocktail truss tomatoes
- 12 French-trimmed lamb cutlets
- Fresh mint leaves, to serve
- 3/4 cup fresh mint leaves, finely chopped
- 3/4 teaspoons caster sugar
- 1 1/2 tablespoons boiling water
- 1 teaspoon finely grated lemon rind
- 2 tablespoons white balsamic vinegar

Direction

- Preheat oven to 200°C/180°C fan forced. Line a baking tray with baking paper. Place potato in a saucepan. Cover with water. Bring to boil over medium-high heat. Season with salt. Cook for 15 minutes or until almost tender. Add peas. Cook for a further 2 minutes or until tender. Drain. Return to pan. Add shallot and milk. Mash until smooth. Stir through spinach until just wilted. Season. Keep warm.
- Meanwhile, place tomatoes on prepared tray. Spray with olive oil. Season. Roast for 10 minutes or until just starting to collapse.
- For the mint sauce, place mint and sugar in a heatproof bowl. Pour over boiling water. Stir to dissolve sugar. Stir in lemon rind and vinegar. Season.
- Heat a large non-stick frying pan over medium-high heat. Spray cutlets with olive oil. Season. Cook in 2 batches, turning, for 3-4 minutes for medium or until cooked to your liking. Rest for 2 minutes. Serve with mash, tomatoes and mint sauce, and sprinkle with mint leaves.

Nutrition Information

- Calories: 356.827 calories
- Saturated Fat: 3 grams saturated fat
- Total Carbohydrate: 28 grams carbohydrates
- Protein: 35 grams protein
- Total Fat: 9 grams fat

95. Lamb Cutlets With Haloumi

Serving: 4 | Prep: 35mins | Ready in: 43mins

Ingredients

- 3 cloves garlic, finely chopped

- 1/2 teaspoon smoked paprika or sweet paprika
- 1 tablespoon Greek oregano, crumbled
- Zest and juice of 1 lemon, (plus extra lemon wedges to serve)
- 12 (700g) lamb cutlets, french trimmed
- 1/4 cup (60ml) extra virgin olive oil
- 250g haloumi, cut into 12 slices
- 12 slices of Italian-style bread, lightly toasted
- 2 egg tomatoes, cut into 12 slices
- 2 tablespoons fresh oregano leaves

Direction

- Combine 1 teaspoon salt, garlic, paprika, Greek oregano, lemon rind and 1/2 the juice in a shallow dish. Add lamb and turn to coat. Cover and refrigerate for 30 minutes.
- Preheat oven to 220°C. Heat 1 tablespoon olive oil in a large frying pan over medium heat. Cook haloumi, in 2 batches, for 30 seconds each side or until golden. Heat 1 tablespoon oil in same pan over high heat and cook cutlets, in 2 batches, for 30-45 seconds each side or until browned. Arrange bread, tomatoes, cutlets and haloumi, alternately and slightly overlapping, in a baking dish. Drizzle with remaining oil and lemon juice, scatter with fresh oregano leaves and bake in oven for 10 minutes or until tomato is soft. Serve with lemon wedges.

Nutrition Information

- Calories: 773.165 calories
- Total Carbohydrate: 42 grams carbohydrates
- Sugar: 5 grams sugar
- Sodium: 2310.94 milligrams sodium
- Total Fat: 42 grams fat
- Saturated Fat: 15 grams saturated fat
- Protein: 56 grams protein
- Cholesterol: 150 milligrams cholesterol

96. Lamb Cutlets With Lentil Salad

Serving: 4 | Prep: 5mins | Ready in: 15mins

Ingredients

- 2 tablespoons olive oil
- 2 garlic cloves, crushed
- 2 x 400g cans brown lentils, drained, rinsed
- 80g baby spinach
- 60g feta
- 12 French-trimmed lamb cutlets
- 2 teaspoons lemon pepper seasoning

Direction

- Heat 1 tablespoon of oil in a non-stick frying pan over medium heat. Add garlic and lentils. Cook, stirring occasionally, for 3 to 4 minutes or until lentils are heated through. Remove to a bowl. Add spinach. Crumble over feta. Stir until just combined. Season with salt and pepper. Cover to keep warm.
- Add remaining oil to the hot frying pan. Cook cutlets, in batches, for 2 to 3 minutes each side for medium or until cooked to your liking. Sprinkle the seasoning over both sides of the cutlets.
- Spoon lentil salad onto plates. Top with cutlets and serve.

Nutrition Information

- Calories: 498.793 calories
- Saturated Fat: 10 grams saturated fat
- Protein: 46 grams protein
- Cholesterol: 130 milligrams cholesterol
- Sodium: 316.3 milligrams sodium
- Total Fat: 29 grams fat
- Total Carbohydrate: 12 grams carbohydrates
- Sugar: 1 grams sugar

97. Lamb Cutlets With Lentil Salad And Mint And Watercress Pesto

Serving: 4 | Prep: 10mins | Ready in: 35mins

Ingredients

- 200g watercress
- 2 cups mint leaves
- 2 tablespoons pine nuts, toasted
- 1 garlic clove
- 1/3 cup (25g) parmesan, grated
- 1 tablespoon lemon juice
- 1/3 cup (80ml) olive oil, plus extra to brush
- 100g whole green Puy-style lentils
- 2 zucchini, sliced into rounds
- 1/2 cup (75g) sun-dried tomatoes in oil, drained
- 150g marinated feta, crumbled
- 12 French-trimmed lamb cutlets

Direction

- Place 100g watercress in a food processor with the mint, pine nuts, garlic, parmesan and lemon juice and whiz to combine. With the motor running, gradually add olive oil until smooth. Season and set aside.
- Cook the lentils in a saucepan of boiling water over medium-high heat for 15 minutes or until tender, then drain.
- Meanwhile, preheat a barbecue or chargrill pan to medium-high. Brush zucchini with oil and cook for 1 minute each side or until tender and charred.
- Place zucchini in a bowl with lentils, sun-dried tomatoes, feta and remaining 100g watercress. Add half the pesto and toss to combine.
- Brush lamb with oil, season and chargrill for 2 minutes each side for medium-rare or until cooked to your liking. Serve cutlets with the lentil salad and remaining pesto.

98. Lamb Cutlets With Minted Potato Salad

Serving: 4 | Prep: 30mins | Ready in: 60mins

Ingredients

- 8 heart smart lamb cutlets
- 1 tablespoon olive oil
- 1 lemon, rind finely grated, juiced
- 2 garlic cloves, crushed
- 80g mixed green salad leaves, to serve
- Minted potato salad
- 750g Desiree potatoes
- 1 small red onion, halved, thinly sliced
- 1/2 cup reduced-fat yoghurt
- 1/4 cup light sour cream
- 1/2 cup mint leaves, shredded

Direction

- Place lamb into a shallow ceramic dish. Combine oil, lemon rind, lemon juice and garlic in a jug. Whisk to combine. Pour over lamb. Turn to coat. Cover. Refrigerate for 30 minutes, if time permits.
- Make minted potato salad: Wash potatoes. Cut into 3cm cubes. Place into a large saucepan. Cover with cold water. Bring to the boil over high heat. Reduce heat to medium. Cook for 15 minutes or until just tender. Drain. Set aside to cool slightly.
- Mix together onion, yoghurt, sour cream, mint, and salt and pepper in a small bowl. Add to potatoes. Stir gently to combine.
- Preheat barbecue plate on high heat until hot. Reduce heat to medium-high. Cook lamb for 3 minutes each side for medium or until cooked to your liking. Serve lamb with potato salad and green salad leaves.

Nutrition Information

- Calories: 0
- Saturated Fat: 6.8 grams saturated fat
- Total Carbohydrate: 29.9 grams carbohydrates
- Sodium: 107 milligrams sodium

- Total Fat: 16.3 grams fat
- Protein: 26.3 grams protein

99. Lamb Cutlets With Nam Jim And Coconut Rice

Serving: 4 | Prep: 20mins | Ready in: 45mins

Ingredients

- 12 French-trimmed lamb cutlets
- Rice bran oil cooking spray
- Steamed baby bok choy, to serve
- 2 long green chillies, roughly chopped
- 2 garlic cloves, quartered
- 2 green onions, roughly chopped
- 2 tablespoons lime juice
- 1 1/2 tablespoons Chang's fish sauce
- 2 tablespoons grated palm sugar
- 1/4 cup chopped fresh coriander leaves
- 1 1/2 cups jasmine rice
- 400ml can coconut milk
- 1/2 teaspoon salt
- 1/3 cup chopped fresh coriander leaves

Direction

- Make Nam Jim: Place chilli, garlic, onion, lime juice, fish sauce, sugar and coriander in a food processor. Process until almost smooth.
- Make Coconut rice: Rinse rice under cold water until water runs clear. Drain. Place rice, coconut milk, salt and 1 cup cold water in a heavy-based saucepan over medium heat. Bring to the boil, stirring occasionally. Reduce heat to low. Simmer, covered, for 20 minutes or until rice is tender. Remove from heat. Stand, covered, for 5 minutes. Fluff rice with a fork. Stir in coriander.
- Meanwhile, heat a chargrill pan over medium-high heat. Lightly spray lamb with oil. Season with salt and freshly ground black pepper. Cook lamb for 3 to 4 minutes each side for medium or until cooked to your liking.
- Serve cutlets with rice, steamed greens and topped with Nam Jim.

Nutrition Information

- Calories: 743.051 calories
- Sugar: 9 grams sugar
- Sodium: 1144.6 milligrams sodium
- Saturated Fat: 21 grams saturated fat
- Protein: 42 grams protein
- Cholesterol: 121 milligrams cholesterol
- Total Fat: 32 grams fat
- Total Carbohydrate: 70 grams carbohydrates

100. Lamb Cutlets With Orzo And Eggplant

Serving: 4 | Prep: 15mins | Ready in: 27mins

Ingredients

- 8 (550g) lamb cutlets, frenched*
- Juice of 2 lemons
- 1 clove garlic, finely chopped
- 100ml Colavita olive oil
- 1 tablespoon tomato paste
- 1 (450g) large eggplant, cut into 1cm-thick slices
- 350g orzo (risoni)*
- 1/2 bunch flat-leaf parsley, coarsely chopped
- 1/4 cup coriander leaves
- 4 green onions, thinly sliced
- 1/3 cup (50g) pine nuts, lightly roasted
- Tzatziki (see 'Quick dip'), to serve

Direction

- Preheat a barbecue to medium-high heat. Place lamb in a bowl. Add 1/4 lemon juice, garlic and 1 tablespoon oil. Season to taste with salt and pepper then toss well to combine. In a large bowl, whisk together tomato paste, 2 tablespoons oil and another 1/4 lemon juice.

Add eggplant. Season to taste and toss well to combine.
- Cook orzo in a large saucepan of boiling salted water for 11 minutes or until al dente. Drain then return to pan. Add herbs, onions, pine nuts, remaining oil and lemon juice. Season to taste and combine well.
- Meanwhile, barbecue lamb for 2 1/2 minutes each side for medium-rare, then set aside in a warm place to rest. Barbecue eggplant for 2 minutes each side or until tender. Layer eggplant and orzo among 4 plates. Top with cutlets. Serve with tzatziki.

Nutrition Information

- Calories: 848.45 calories
- Sugar: 5 grams sugar
- Cholesterol: 92 milligrams cholesterol
- Total Carbohydrate: 67 grams carbohydrates
- Total Fat: 45 grams fat
- Saturated Fat: 8 grams saturated fat
- Protein: 39 grams protein
- Sodium: 133.57 milligrams sodium

101. Lamb Cutlets With Pistachio And Mint Pesto

Serving: 4 | Prep: 15mins | Ready in: 25mins

Ingredients

- 6 kipfler potatoes, thickly sliced diagonally
- 12 lamb cutlets
- 170g jar marinated artichokes, drained, halved
- 1 red onion, thinly sliced
- 1/2 cup fresh flat-leaf parsley leaves
- 1/4 cup fresh mint leaves
- 1 tablespoon extra virgin olive oil
- 1 tablespoon lemon juice
- 1/3 cup pistachio kernels, toasted
- 1/4 cup finely grated parmesan
- 1 garlic clove, finely chopped
- 1 cup fresh mint leaves
- 1/3 cup extra virgin olive oil

Direction

- Make pistachio and mint pesto. Process pistachios, parmesan, garlic and mint in a food processor until finely chopped. With motor running, gradually add oil in a thin, steady stream until mixture is well combined. Season with salt and pepper.
- Place potato in a large saucepan and cover with cold water. Place over high heat. Bring to the boil. Cook for 10 minutes or until tender. Drain. Rinse under cold water. Drain.
- Meanwhile, heat a large, non-stick frying pan over high heat. Add lamb. Cook for 2 to 3 minutes each side for medium or until cooked to your liking. Transfer to a plate. Cover loosely with foil. Set aside for 5 minutes.
- Place potato in a large bowl. Add artichokes, onion, parsley, mint, oil and lemon juice. Season with salt and pepper. Gently toss to combine.
- Divide potato mixture among serving plates. Top with lamb and dollop with pesto. Serve.

Nutrition Information

- Calories: 643.388 calories
- Protein: 37 grams protein
- Sodium: 394 milligrams sodium
- Total Fat: 43.1 grams fat
- Saturated Fat: 9.8 grams saturated fat
- Total Carbohydrate: 24.3 grams carbohydrates
- Cholesterol: 93 milligrams cholesterol

102. Lamb Cutlets With Pistachio Pesto

Serving: 4 | Prep: 10mins | Ready in: 14mins

Ingredients

- 100g pistachio kernels

- 30g fresh white breadcrumbs
- 1 lemon, rind grated
- 1 garlic clove, crushed
- 25g grated parmesan
- 1/2 cup firmly packed fresh basil leaves
- 120ml olive oil
- 12 Frenched lamb cutlets

Direction

- Place the pistachios, breadcrumbs, lemon rind, garlic, parmesan, basil and 100ml olive oil in a food processor and process to a paste. Season with salt and pepper.
- Heat a chargrill to high, brush the cutlets with the remaining oil and chargrill for 1-2 minutes each side. Serve with the pistachio pesto.

Nutrition Information

- Calories: 720.824 calories
- Total Carbohydrate: 7 grams carbohydrates
- Sugar: 2 grams sugar
- Protein: 43 grams protein
- Cholesterol: 126 milligrams cholesterol
- Sodium: 259.17 milligrams sodium
- Total Fat: 58 grams fat
- Saturated Fat: 13 grams saturated fat

103. Lamb Cutlets With Radish Salad Cinnamon Yoghurt

Serving: 4 | Prep: 30mins | Ready in: 40mins

Ingredients

- 1/2 small red onion, thinly sliced
- 1/2 teaspoon sumac
- 1 garlic clove, crushed
- 2 tablespoons olive oil
- 2 tablespoons fresh lemon juice
- 3 carrots, peeled
- 5 radishes, ends trimmed, thinly sliced
- 1 cup fresh continental parsley leaves
- 1 cup fresh mint leaves, coarsely chopped
- 65g (1/3 cup) sultanas
- 45g (1/4 cup) toasted pine nuts
- 1 tablespoon sweet paprika
- 1 tablespoon ground cumin
- 12 lamb cutlets, French trimmed
- Olive oil, extra, to grease
- 130g (1/2 cup) natural yoghurt
- 1/2 teaspoon ground cinnamon

Direction

- Place the onion in a small bowl and cover with cold water. Set aside for 1 hour to soak. Drain. Place the onion and sumac in a large bowl. Toss to coat.
- Combine the garlic, half the oil and half the lemon juice in a small bowl. Peel the carrots lengthways into ribbons. Add the carrot, radish, parsley, mint, sultanas and pine nuts to the onion mixture. Drizzle over the garlic mixture. Gently toss until just combined.
- Combine the paprika, cumin and the remaining oil in a small bowl. Brush both sides of the lamb with the paprika mixture. Brush a barbecue grill or chargrill with extra oil to grease. Cook the lamb on grill for 2-3 minutes each side for medium or until cooked to your liking. Transfer to a plate. Cover with foil and set aside for 3 minutes to rest.
- Meanwhile, combine the yoghurt, cinnamon and remaining lemon juice in a bowl. Season with salt and pepper.
- Divide salad and lamb among serving plates. Serve with the yoghurt mixture.

Nutrition Information

- Calories: 566.43 calories
- Cholesterol: 126 milligrams cholesterol
- Sodium: 176.25 milligrams sodium
- Saturated Fat: 9 grams saturated fat
- Total Carbohydrate: 19 grams carbohydrates
- Sugar: 18 grams sugar
- Total Fat: 36 grams fat

- Protein: 40 grams protein
- Sugar: 1 grams sugar
- Sodium: 423.39 milligrams sodium
- Saturated Fat: 12 grams saturated fat
- Total Carbohydrate: 32 grams carbohydrates

104. Lamb Cutlets With Risoni Salad

Serving: 4 | Prep: 15mins | Ready in: 21mins

Ingredients

- 165g (3/4 cup) risoni pasta
- 2 tablespoons olive oil
- 1 1/2 tablespoons red wine vinegar
- 1 teaspoon Dijon mustard
- Salt and cracked black pepper
- 8-12 lamb cutlets
- 125g cherry tomatoes, halved
- 1/4 cup roughly torn basil leaves
- 1/2 cup (100g) crumbled feta
- 2 tablespoons pine nuts, toasted

Direction

- Cook the risoni in a large saucepan of salted boiling water according to packet instructions. Drain and set aside.
- Meanwhile, place the oil, vinegar, mustard, salt and pepper in a bowl and whisk until well combined. Set aside.
- Heat a barbecue or grill to high. Sprinkle lamb cutlets with salt and pepper and brush with a little oil. Cook for 3 minutes each side or until cooking to your liking. Remove, cover and set aside.
- Combine the risoni in a large bowl with the tomato, basil, feta and pine nuts. Drizzle with the dressing and toss gently to combine. To serve, divide risoni among serving plates and top with several cutlets.

Nutrition Information

- Calories: 633.111 calories
- Protein: 45 grams protein
- Total Fat: 36 grams fat

105. Lamb Cutlets With Roast Beetroot Salad Caraway Dressing

Serving: 4 | Prep: 20mins | Ready in: 70mins

Ingredients

- 1 bunch baby beetroot, roots and stems trimmed
- 1 bunch spring onions, roots trimmed, stems cut to 5cm
- 1 tablespoon olive oil
- 100g baby rocket leaves
- Olive oil, to grease
- 12 lamb cutlets, French trimmed
- 1 x 150g pkt goat's cheese, crumbled
- 1 tablespoon caraway seeds
- 80ml (1/3 cup) olive oil
- 2 tablespoons balsamic vinegar
- 2 tablespoons chopped fresh oregano
- 1 tablespoon wholegrain mustard
- 1 garlic clove, crushed
- Salt freshly ground black pepper

Direction

- Preheat oven to 200°C. Wrap each individual beetroot in foil and place in a roasting pan. Bake in preheated oven for 30 minutes. Remove from oven, add the spring onions to the pan and drizzle with the oil. Cook for a further 15 minutes or until the beetroot is tender and the onions are brown. Remove from oven and set aside for 5 minutes to cool.
- Meanwhile, to make the caraway dressing, heat a non-stick frying pan over medium heat. Add caraway seeds and cook, stirring, for 2 minutes or until fragrant. Remove from heat

and place in a jug. Add the oil, vinegar, oregano, mustard and garlic and stir to combine. Taste and season with salt and pepper.
- Wearing rubber gloves to avoid staining your hands, peel beetroot and cut in half. Place in a bowl. Add spring onions, rocket and half the caraway dressing and gently toss to combine.
- Preheat a chargrill over medium-high heat. Brush with oil to lightly grease. Cook cutlets for 2 minutes each side for medium-rare or to your liking.
- Divide beetroot salad among serving plates and top with goat's cheese and cutlets. Drizzle with remaining caraway dressing and serve immediately.

Nutrition Information

- Calories: 623.312 calories
- Total Fat: 47 grams fat
- Total Carbohydrate: 6 grams carbohydrates
- Sugar: 5 grams sugar
- Cholesterol: 138 milligrams cholesterol
- Saturated Fat: 15 grams saturated fat
- Protein: 44 grams protein
- Sodium: 359.04 milligrams sodium

106. Lamb Cutlets With Spiced Carrot Salad

Serving: 4 | Prep: 25mins | Ready in: 31mins

Ingredients

- 3 cups coarsely grated carrot (about 3 carrots)
- 400g can chickpeas, drained, rinsed
- 1/2 cup continental parsley leaves
- 3 radishes, thinly sliced
- 1/2 cup (95g) raisins
- Freshly ground pepper
- 2 tablespoons orange juice
- 1/4 teaspoon ground cinnamon
- 2 teaspoons olive oil
- 2 teaspoons dried mint flakes
- 2 teaspoons ground cumin
- 8 trimmed lamb cutlets

Direction

- Combine the carrot, chickpeas, parsley leaves, radish, raisins and pepper in a bowl. Mix the orange juice and cinnamon together. Add to salad and toss well.
- Mix the olive oil, mint and cumin. Brush the cutlets with the mixture.
- Cook the cutlets in a frying pan over a medium-high heat for 3 minutes each side. Set aside, covered with foil, for 3 minutes to rest. Serve the cutlets with the carrot salad.

Nutrition Information

- Calories: 391.243 calories
- Total Carbohydrate: 32 grams carbohydrates
- Sugar: 23 grams sugar
- Cholesterol: 80 milligrams cholesterol
- Sodium: 275.26 milligrams sodium
- Saturated Fat: 5 grams saturated fat
- Total Fat: 15 grams fat
- Protein: 29 grams protein

107. Lamb Cutlets With Spicy Parsnip Chips And Almond Sauce

Serving: 4 | Prep: 10mins | Ready in: 40mins

Ingredients

- 8 small (about 750g) parsnips, peeled, quartered
- 2 tablespoons extra virgin olive oil
- 1 tablespoon fresh rosemary leaves
- 1 teaspoon ground cumin, plus extra, to sprinkle
- 1/2 teaspoon dried chilli flakes
- 1 lemon, rind finely grated

- 60g (1/3 cup) blanched almonds, lightly toasted
- 130g (1/2 cup) reduced-fat Greek yoghurt
- 1 tablespoon apple cider vinegar
- 1 tablespoon water
- 1 teaspoon maple syrup
- 8 French-trimmed lamb cutlets
- Broccolini, steamed, to serve

Direction

- Preheat oven to 210C/190C fan forced. Line a baking tray with baking paper. Place the parsnips on prepared tray. Drizzle with oil. Sprinkle with the rosemary, cumin and chilli. Season well. Toss to coat. Roast, stirring halfway, for 30 minutes or until browned and tender.
- Meanwhile, cut two-thirds of the lemon into 4 wedges. Juice the remaining lemon. Process the almonds in a food processor until finely ground. Add the yoghurt, vinegar, water, syrup, lemon rind and juice. Process until smooth. Season.
- Heat a non-stick frying pan over medium-high heat. Spray lamb with oil and season. Cook, turning, for 3 minutes for medium or until cooked to your liking. Transfer to a plate and rest for 3 minutes. Divide sauce, lamb, parsnip and broccolini among plates. Sprinkle with extra cumin. Serve with lemon.

Nutrition Information

- Calories: 473.459 calories
- Total Fat: 25 grams fat
- Total Carbohydrate: 26 grams carbohydrates
- Saturated Fat: 5 grams saturated fat
- Protein: 29 grams protein

108. Lamb Cutlets With Tomato Salsa

Serving: 4 | Prep: 5mins | Ready in: 27mins

Ingredients

- 4 large desiree potatoes, thickly sliced
- 1 tablespoon red wine vinegar
- 2 tablespoons olive oil
- 3 tomatoes, roughly chopped
- 1/2 small red onion, finely chopped
- 1/4 cup fresh basil leaves, shredded
- 1/4 cup pine nuts, toasted
- 8 lamb cutlets, trimmed

Direction

- Place potato in a heatproof, microwave safe bowl. Add 2 tablespoons cold water. Cover with plastic wrap. Microwave on high (100%) for 8 minutes or until tender. Drain.
- Meanwhile, combine vinegar and 1 1/2 tablespoons oil in a large bowl. Add tomato, onion, basil and pine nuts. Season with salt and pepper. Toss to combine.
- Heat remaining oil in a large, non-stick frying pan over medium-high heat. Cook lamb, in batches, for 3 to 4 minutes each side for medium or until cooked to your liking. Transfer to a plate. Cover with foil.
- Add potato to pan. Cook for 2 to 3 minutes each side or until golden. Divide potato between plates. Top with cutlets and tomato mixture. Serve.

Nutrition Information

- Calories: 444.54 calories
- Protein: 26.9 grams protein
- Saturated Fat: 5.8 grams saturated fat
- Cholesterol: 65 milligrams cholesterol
- Sodium: 135 milligrams sodium
- Total Fat: 25.7 grams fat
- Total Carbohydrate: 23.3 grams carbohydrates

109. Lamb Cutlets With Warm Roasted Capsicum Salsa

Serving: 4 | Prep: 25mins | Ready in: 45mins

Ingredients

- 1 red capsicum, halved, seeded
- 1 yellow capsicum, halved, seeded
- 60ml (1/4 cup) extra virgin olive oil
- 2 zucchinis, trimmed, finely chopped
- 2 cloves garlic, finely chopped
- 40g (1/4 cup) pitted Kalamata olives, finely chopped
- 1 tablespoon baby capers
- 2 tablespoons thyme leaves
- 80ml (1/3 cup) balsamic vinegar
- 1 tablespoon brown sugar
- 12 (600g) French-trimmed lamb cutlets
- 100g baby rocket leaves

Direction

- Preheat grill to high. Grill capsicums, skin-side up, for 10 minutes or until charred and blistered. Transfer to a heatproof bowl, cover with plastic wrap and set aside for 5 minutes. Once cooled, peel and discard skins and finely chop flesh. Place in a large bowl.
- Meanwhile, heat oil in a large frying pan over medium heat. Add zucchinis and garlic, and cook, stirring, for 3 minutes or until zucchinis are just tender. Remove from heat. Add to capsicum with olives, capers and thyme. Season with salt and freshly ground black pepper, then cover.
- Place vinegar and sugar in a small frying pan over high heat. Bring to the boil. Cook, stirring occasionally, for 2 minutes or until syrupy and reduced by half.
- Heat a chargrill pan over high heat. Season cutlets. Chargrill for 2 minutes each side for medium-rare or until cooked to your liking. Transfer to a plate and cover with foil. Rest for 5 minutes.
- Divide rocket among plates and spoon over some of the capsicum salsa. Top with cutlets, drizzle with vinegar sauce and top with remaining salsa to serve.

Nutrition Information

- Calories: 410.602 calories
- Sodium: 231.09 milligrams sodium
- Total Fat: 28 grams fat
- Total Carbohydrate: 8 grams carbohydrates
- Sugar: 6 grams sugar
- Protein: 31 grams protein
- Cholesterol: 100 milligrams cholesterol
- Saturated Fat: 7 grams saturated fat

110. Lamb Cutlets With Whipped Feta And Carrot Pickle

Serving: 4 | Prep: 12mins | Ready in: 20mins

Ingredients

- 3 carrots, peeled
- 2 tablespoons lemon juice
- 2 teaspoons brown sugar
- 1/2 cup fresh coriander leaves
- 75g reduced-fat fresh ricotta
- 50g low-fat feta
- 2 tablespoons skim milk
- Extra virgin olive oil, to drizzle (optional)
- 12 (about 660g) French-trimmed lamb cutlets
- 2 teaspoon ground sumac
- 98% fat-free wholemeal pita bread, warmed, to serve

Direction

- Process the carrots in a food processor until finely grated. Whisk the lemon juice and brown sugar together in a glass or ceramic bowl. Season well. Add the carrot and coriander. Toss well to combine. Set aside for 10 minutes to develop the flavours.

- Meanwhile, process the ricotta, feta and milk until smooth and combined. Transfer to a bowl. Drizzle with a little oil, if using.
- Heat a non-stick frying pan over medium-high heat. Spray lamb with olive oil. Sprinkle with the sumac and season. Cook, in 2 batches, for 2 minutes each side for medium or until cooked to your liking. Transfer to a plate. Rest for 2 minutes.
- Divide the carrot pickle, whipped feta and lamb among plates. Serve with pita.

111. Lamb Cutlets With White Wine And Rosemary

Serving: 4 | Prep: 13mins | Ready in: 19mins

Ingredients

- 2 cloves garlic, crushed
- 1 teaspoon finely grated lemon rind
- 1/4 cup white wine
- 1/3 cup olive oil
- 1 tablespoon chopped rosemary
- salt and cracked black pepper
- 12 lamb cutlets, trimmed
- 2 tomatoes, seeded and chopped
- 1/4 cup kalamata olives
- 2 tablespoons feta, crumbled

Direction

- Combine garlic, lemon rind, wine, rosemary, oil, salt and pepper in a bowl. Add cutlets and toss to coat. Cover and refrigerate for 10 minutes.
- Meanwhile, combine tomatoes, olives and feta. Drizzle with olive oil and set aside.
- Heat a grill or hot plate to medium high heat. Cook the cutlets for 3 minutes on each side or until cooked to your liking.
- Serve with tomato salad.

Nutrition Information

- Calories: 505.007 calories
- Total Carbohydrate: 3 grams carbohydrates
- Cholesterol: 125 milligrams cholesterol
- Saturated Fat: 11 grams saturated fat
- Total Fat: 38 grams fat
- Sugar: 2 grams sugar
- Protein: 37 grams protein
- Sodium: 354.3 milligrams sodium

112. Lamb Forequarter Chops With Chickpeas And Spinach

Serving: 4 | Prep: 10mins | Ready in: 100mins

Ingredients

- 4 Coles Australian Lamb Forequarter Chops (about 250g each)
- 2 tablespoons olive oil
- 2 celery stalks, cut into small dice
- 2 spring onions, finely chopped
- 3 garlic cloves, finely chopped
- 3 teaspoons finely chopped fresh rosemary
- 1/2 cup (125ml) dry white wine
- 3/4 cup (185ml) salt-reduced chicken stock
- 400g can chickpeas, rinsed, drained
- 60g fresh spinach, coarsely chopped
- 1/3 cup (95g) Greek-style yoghurt
- Extra virgin olive oil, for drizzling

Direction

- Preheat oven to 150C (130C fan-forced). Season lamb with salt and pepper. Heat a large heavy ovenproof sauté pan over high heat and add olive oil. When oil is hot, add lamb and cook for 4 mins each side or until brown on both sides. Transfer lamb to a plate.
- Pour off all but 1 tablespoon oil from pan. Reduce heat to medium. Add celery, spring onions, garlic, rosemary, 1 tsp. salt and ½ tsp. pepper. Cook, stirring, for 1 min or until fragrant. Add wine and boil for 1 min. Add stock and bring to a simmer. Return lamb to pan. Cover tightly. Transfer to oven and braise

- for 1¼ hours or until lamb is fork-tender. Transfer lamb to a heavy baking tray, reserving the braising liquid in the pan.
- Preheat grill on high. Place baking tray under grill for 3 mins or until lamb is browned and crisp. Rest lamb briefly.
- Meanwhile, stir chickpeas into reserved braising liquid in the pan and simmer for 5 mins or until liquid reduces by half. Remove from heat. Stir in spinach. Season with salt and pepper.
- Divide chickpea mixture and lamb among 4 plates. Serve with yoghurt drizzled with extra virgin olive oil.

Nutrition Information

- Calories: 369.255 calories
- Protein: 18 grams protein
- Sodium: 998 milligrams sodium
- Total Fat: 23 grams fat
- Saturated Fat: 7 grams saturated fat
- Total Carbohydrate: 14 grams carbohydrates
- Sugar: 4 grams sugar

113. Lamb Loin Chops With Peppered Mash And Kale Salad

Serving: 4 | Prep: 20mins | Ready in: 35mins

Ingredients

- 800g potatoes, peeled, coarsely chopped
- 2 garlic cloves, crushed
- 1 teaspoon cracked black pepper
- 3 teaspoons fresh thyme leaves
- 2 spring onions, thinly sliced
- 1/4 cup (60ml) milk
- 80g cream cheese
- 8 Coles Australian Lamb Loin Chops
- 300g green beans, trimmed
- 200g pkt Coles Kale Beetroot Salad Kit

Direction

- Cook the potato in a large saucepan of boiling salted water for 15 mins or until just tender. Drain. Return potato to pan and mash until smooth. Add garlic, pepper, thyme, onion, milk and cream cheese. Stir to combine.
- Meanwhile, spray a barbecue plate or chargrill pan with olive oil spray. Heat over medium-high heat. Cook lamb for 3-4 mins each side for medium or until cooked to your liking. Transfer to a plate and set aside for 5 mins to rest.
- Cook the beans in a saucepan of salted boiling water for 2 mins or until bright green and tender crisp. Refresh under cold running water. Drain.
- Prepare kale salad following packet directions. Divide lamb, mash, beans and salad among serving plates to serve.

114. Lamb Neck Chops With Vegetables

Serving: 6 | Prep: 10mins | Ready in: 250mins

Ingredients

- 1/2 cup plain flour
- 2kg lamb neck chops
- 2 tablespoons olive oil
- 2 leeks, trimmed, washed, thinly sliced
- 2 large carrots, peeled, cut into 2cm pieces
- 3 small parsnips, peeled, core removed, cut into 2cm pieces
- 2 cups Massel chicken style liquid stock
- 1/3 cup tarragon leaves, roughly chopped
- mashed potato, to serve

Direction

- Place flour in a shallow dish. Season with salt and pepper. Lightly coat chops in flour.
- Heat oil in a large, deep frying pan over medium-high heat. Cook chops, in batches, for 3 minutes each side or until browned. Transfer to a plate, cover and set aside. Add leeks,

carrots and parsnips to pan. Cook, stirring occasionally, for 3 to 4 minutes or until tender. Add stock and bring to the boil. Remove from heat.
- Spoon vegetables and stock mixture into slow cooker. Place chops on top. Cover and cook on HIGH for 3 to 4 hours or until meat is tender and sauce is thick. Stir in tarragon. Serve with mashed potato.

Nutrition Information

- Calories: 503.573 calories
- Total Fat: 22 grams fat
- Cholesterol: 171 milligrams cholesterol
- Total Carbohydrate: 14 grams carbohydrates
- Sugar: 3 grams sugar
- Protein: 61 grams protein
- Sodium: 518.45 milligrams sodium
- Saturated Fat: 6 grams saturated fat

115. Lamb Rack With Grilled Sweet Potato Salad And Olive Chimichurri

Serving: 4 | Prep: 20mins | Ready in: 50mins

Ingredients

- 105g (1/2 cup) French green lentils
- 2 (about 480g each) lamb racks, French trimmed
- 400g sweet potato, thinly sliced
- 1 red onion, cut into wedges
- 80ml (1/3 cup) extra virgin olive oil
- 300g Swiss brown mushrooms, halved
- 1 tablespoon red wine vinegar
- 85g (1/2 cup) pitted Sicilian olives
- 1 cup firmly packed fresh parsley leaves
- 1/3 cup fresh coriander leaves
- 2 tablespoons fresh oregano leaves
- 2 garlic cloves, chopped
- 1/2 teaspoons dried chilli flakes
- 125ml (1/2 cup) extra virgin olive oil
- 1 1/2 tablespoons red wine vinegar

Direction

- Preheat oven to 200C/180C fan forced. Line a baking tray with baking paper. Rinse lentils. Cook lentils in a saucepan of boiling water following packet directions until just tender. Drain. Refresh under cold running water. Place in a large bowl.
- Heat a frying pan over medium-high heat. Spray lamb with olive oil. Season. Cook, turning, for 5 minutes, until browned. Transfer to the prepared tray. Roast for 12-14 minutes for medium or until cooked to your liking. Cover loosely with foil. Leave for 10 minutes to rest. Halve racks.
- Meanwhile, preheat a barbecue grill on medium. Combine potato, onion and 2 tbsp. oil in a large bowl. Season. Combine mushroom and 1 tbsp. oil in a bowl. Season. Cook the potato mixture, turning, for 6 minutes. Add the mushroom and cook for a further 6 minutes or until charred and tender. Add to lentils in bowl.
- For the chimichurri, process olives, parsley, coriander, oregano, garlic and chilli until finely chopped. With the motor running, add the oil and vinegar in a steady stream until smooth and combined. Season.
- Add vinegar, 1/3 cup chimichurri and remaining 1 tbsp. oil to lentil mixture. Gently toss to combine. Divide among plates. Serve with lamb and remaining chimichurri.

Nutrition Information

- Calories: 841.28 calories
- Protein: 38 grams protein
- Total Fat: 61 grams fat
- Saturated Fat: 12 grams saturated fat
- Total Carbohydrate: 29 grams carbohydrates

116. Lamb Tray Bake With Pesto, Tomatoes And Olives

Serving: 6 | Prep: 10mins | Ready in: 45mins

Ingredients

- 6 (1.2kg) Coles Australian lamb forequarter chops
- 1/2 cup (75g) semi-dried tomatoes, drained, coarsely chopped
- 1/2 cup(130g) Coles Brand Basil Pesto
- 1/2 cup (125ml) chicken stock, warmed
- 1/2 cup (75g) pitted kalamata olives
- 2 x 400g cans Coles Brand cannellini beans, rinsed, drained
- 1/3 cup basil leaves
- Steamed green beans, to serve
- Crusty bread, to serve
- Pesto, extra, to serve

Direction

- Preheat oven to 200C. Preheat a lightly oiled barbecue grill or chargrill on medium-high. Season the chops and cook, in batches, for 2 mins each side or until browned. Place in a large baking tray.
- Add the tomato to the tray. Combine the pesto and stock and pour over the chops. Bake for 10 mins. Baste the chops with the sauce. Add the olives and cannellini beans. Bake for a further 10 mins or until chops are cooked through. Sprinkle with basil leaves.
- Divide tray bake among serving plates and spoon over the sauce. Serve with beans, crusty bread and an extra dollop of pesto.

117. Lamb Wellington Pops With Minted Pea Smash

Serving: 4 | Prep: 40mins | Ready in: 40mins

Ingredients

- 8 lamb cutlets, French trimmed
- 4 sheets frozen puff pastry, partially thawed
- 40g quince paste, cut into 5g slices
- 1 egg, lightly whisked
- 30g butter
- 2 French shallots, finely chopped
- 450g (3 cups) frozen peas
- 2/3 cup fresh mint leaves, chopped
- 2 tablespoons creme fraiche

Direction

- Preheat oven to 220°C/200°C fan forced. Heat a large non-stick frying pan over high heat. Spray lamb with oil. Season. Cook, in 2 batches, or 30 seconds each side or until browned. Transfer to a plate lined with paper towel.
- Use a 9cm round cutter to cut 8 discs from pastry. Use a 10cm round cutter to cut 8 discs from remaining pastry. Divide the 9cm discs among 2 lined baking trays. Top each round with a lamb cutlet and a slice of quince paste. Top each cutlet with a 10cm disc. Press to seal and crimp the edges. Brush with egg. Season with pepper. Bake for 14 minutes or until golden.
- Meanwhile, for pea smash, heat butter in the frying pan over medium heat. Add shallot and stir for 2 minutes or until soft. Stir in peas for 5 minutes or until tender. Cool for 2 minutes. Stir in mint and crème fraiche. Season. Use a potato masher to coarsely mash.
- Divide among plates and top with lamb.

Nutrition Information

- Calories: 696.685 calories
- Protein: 33 grams protein
- Saturated Fat: 22 grams saturated fat
- Total Carbohydrate: 48 grams carbohydrates
- Total Fat: 40 grams fat

118. Lamb With Green Bean Salad

Serving: 4 | Prep: 5mins | Ready in: 35mins

Ingredients

- 300g green beans, trimmed
- 50g feta or marinated feta cheese
- 1/2 cup (50g) semi-dried tomatoes, halved
- 1/2 cup Sandhurst pitted kalamata olives
- 2 tablespoons lemon juice
- 4 lamb forequarter chops

Direction

- Cook beans in a saucepan of boiling water for 1 to 2 minutes or until bright green and just tender. Drain. Refresh under cold water.
- Drain feta, reserving 2 tablespoons oil mixture. Place beans, feta, tomatoes and olives in a bowl. Drizzle with lemon juice and reserved oil. Season with salt and pepper. Toss to combine.
- Spray a barbecue plate or chargrill with oil. Heat over medium-high heat. Cook lamb for 4 minutes each side for medium or until cooked to your liking. Serve with bean salad.

Nutrition Information

- Calories: 303.291 calories
- Total Fat: 16.1 grams fat
- Total Carbohydrate: 13.2 grams carbohydrates
- Cholesterol: 66 milligrams cholesterol
- Sodium: 428 milligrams sodium
- Protein: 24 grams protein
- Saturated Fat: 4.6 grams saturated fat

119. Lamb With Grilled Cauliflower Steaks

Serving: 4 | Prep: 20mins | Ready in: 40mins

Ingredients

- 2 tablespoons extra virgin olive oil
- 2 garlic cloves, crushed
- 1 lemon, zested, juiced
- 1 head cauliflower, cut into 1.5cm-thick steaks (see tip)
- 4 Coles Australian Lamb Forequarter Chops
- 1 tablespoon pine nuts, toasted
- 1 tablespoon flaked almonds, toasted
- 1 tablespoon chopped basil
- 1 tablespoon chopped flat-leaf parsley
- 1 tablespoon finely grated parmesan
- Extra virgin olive oil, extra, to serve
- Coles Bakery Stone Baked Pane Di Casa Baguette*, to serve

Direction

- Combine the oil, garlic, lemon zest and lemon juice in a shallow bowl. Add the cauliflower steaks and turn to coat. Season. Transfer cauliflower to a plate. Add the lamb to the oil mixture and turn to coat.
- Preheat a barbecue grill or chargrill on high. Cook the lamb for 4 mins each side for medium or until cooked to your liking. Transfer to a plate. Cover with foil and set aside for 5 mins to rest.
- Cook the cauliflower steaks on the grill for 5 mins each side or until charred and tender.
- Combine the pine nuts, almonds, basil, parsley and parmesan in a bowl. Sprinkle the lamb and cauliflower steaks with the pine nut mixture. Drizzle with a little extra oil and season. Serve with the bread.

120. Lamb With Kale Salad And Creamy Avocado Mint Sauce

Serving: 4 | Prep: 14mins | Ready in: 20mins

Ingredients

- 350g packet kaleslaw kit with seed mix and dressing
- 1 granny smith apple, unpeeled
- 1/3 cup lemon juice
- 1/4 cup extra virgin olive oil
- 12 French-trimmed lamb cutlets
- 1 avocado, halved, roughly chopped
- 2 tablespoons shredded fresh mint leaves, plus extra sprigs to serve
- 8 slices crusty bread, toasted, to serve

Direction

- Remove and set aside seed mix and dressing from slaw kit. Cut apple into matchsticks. Place kale mixture, apple, half the lemon juice and half the oil in a medium bowl. Season with salt and pepper. Toss gently to combine.
- Drizzle remaining oil over lamb. Season with salt and pepper. Heat a chargrill pan or barbecue grill over high heat. Cook lamb for 2 to 3 minutes each side, for medium, or until cooked to your liking.
- Meanwhile, place reserved dressing from kit, avocado, shredded mint, remaining lemon juice and 2 tablespoons water in a small food processor. Season with salt and pepper. Process until smooth.
- Place lamb on a large platter or board with kale salad and bread. Sprinkle salad with reserved seed mix. Sprinkle lamb with extra mint. Serve with sauce.

Nutrition Information

- Calories: 710.786 calories
- Saturated Fat: 8.4 grams saturated fat
- Total Carbohydrate: 54.1 grams carbohydrates
- Protein: 32.6 grams protein
- Cholesterol: 66 milligrams cholesterol
- Sodium: 651 milligrams sodium
- Total Fat: 38.5 grams fat

121. Lamb With Lentil Salad

Serving: 4 | Prep: 15mins | Ready in: 25mins

Ingredients

- 12 Coles Australian Lamb Cutlets
- 2 tablespoons olive oil
- 300g Coles Bakery Rustic Baguette, cut into 3cm-thick slices
- 6 yellow squash, thinly sliced
- 2 x 400g can lentils, rinsed, drained
- 2 teaspoons curry powder
- 1 1/2 cup coriander leaves
- 100g Coles Australian Style Fetta, crumbled

Direction

- Preheat a chargrill plate on high. Combine the lamb cutlets and half the oil in a large bowl. Season. Cook the lamb for 2 mins each side for medium or until cooked to your liking. Transfer to a plate. Cover with foil and set aside for 5 mins to rest.
- Meanwhile, cook the bread on the chargrill for 1 min each side or until lightly charred.
- Heat the remaining oil in a large saucepan over medium heat. Add the squash and cook, stirring, for 3 mins or until just tender. Add the lentils and curry powder and cook for 1-2 mins or until fragrant and heated through. Remove from heat. Stir in the coriander and feta.
- Serve the lamb with the lentil salad and bread.

122. Lamb With Pumpkin And Lentil Winter Salad

Serving: 4 | Prep: 15mins | Ready in: 40mins

Ingredients

- 500g butternut pumpkin, seeded, peeled, cut into 3cm pieces
- 1 bunch Dutch carrots, trimmed

- 1 head broccoli, cut into florets
- 2 teaspoons olive oil
- 1 tablespoon Moroccan seasoning
- 12 Coles Australian Lamb Cutlets, French trimmed (see notes)
- 1/2 cup (140g) Greek-style yoghurt
- 1 tablespoon tahini
- 2 tablespoons lemon juice
- 400g can lentils, drained

Direction

- Preheat oven to 200C. Line a baking tray with baking paper. Combine pumpkin, carrots, broccoli, oil and half the Moroccan seasoning in a large bowl. Arrange in a single layer on the lined tray. Roast, turning occasionally, for 25 mins or until pumpkin is tender.
- Meanwhile, combine lamb and remaining Moroccan seasoning in a bowl. Heat a large frying pan over medium-high heat. Add the lamb and cook for 2-3 mins each side for medium or until cooked to your liking. Transfer to a plate and cover with foil. Set aside for 5 mins to rest.
- Combine the yoghurt, tahini and lemon juice in a small bowl. Season. Combine the pumpkin mixture and lentils in a large bowl. Divide among serving plates. Drizzle with the yoghurt mixture and top with lamb.

Nutrition Information

- Calories: 437.609 calories
- Protein: 36 grams protein
- Total Carbohydrate: 31 grams carbohydrates
- Sugar: 14 grams sugar
- Sodium: 386 milligrams sodium
- Total Fat: 16 grams fat
- Saturated Fat: 5 grams saturated fat

123. Lamb With Roast Pumpkin Salad

Serving: 1 | Prep: 20mins | Ready in: 45mins

Ingredients

- 300g butternut pumpkin, peeled, deseeded, cut into thin wedges
- olive oil cooking spray
- 4 lean lamb cutlets
- 25g baby spinach leaves
- 1 tablespoon pine nuts, toasted
- 50g feta, cut into small cubes
- 2 teaspoons balsamic vinegar
- 2 teaspoons extra virgin olive oil
- 1 garlic clove, crushed

Direction

- Preheat oven to 230°C. Line a baking dish with baking paper. Place pumpkin in a single layer in baking dish. Spray with oil. Season with salt and pepper. Turn pumpkin. Repeat with oil and salt and pepper. Roast for 20 minutes, turning once, until tender.
- Preheat a barbecue grill or chargrill on medium-high heat. Spray both sides of lamb with oil. Season with salt and pepper. Cook for 2 minutes each side for medium or until cooked to your liking. Transfer to a plate. Cover loosely with foil. Stand for 5 minutes.
- Place spinach, pine nuts and feta in a bowl. Toss to combine. Whisk vinegar, oil, garlic and salt and pepper in a jug. Add to salad with pumpkin. Toss gently to combine.
- Serve lamb with roast pumpkin salad.

Nutrition Information

- Calories: 837.217 calories
- Saturated Fat: 18 grams saturated fat
- Protein: 64 grams protein
- Cholesterol: 194 milligrams cholesterol
- Sugar: 17 grams sugar
- Sodium: 712.25 milligrams sodium
- Total Fat: 53 grams fat

- Total Carbohydrate: 23 grams carbohydrates

124. Lamb With Warm Lentil Salad

Serving: 4 | Prep: 20mins | Ready in: 40mins

Ingredients

- 200g punnet grape tomatoes
- 2 teaspoons olive oil
- 1 brown onion, halved, finely chopped
- 2 garlic cloves, crushed
- 1/4 teaspoon cayenne pepper
- 150g cup mushrooms, thickly sliced
- 400g can brown lentils, rinsed, drained
- 1 tablespoon balsamic vinegar
- 40g baby spinach leaves
- 12 (about 975g) lamb cutlets, excess fat trimmed

Direction

- Cut a small slit in each tomato. Heat half the oil in a large non-stick frying pan over medium heat. Add the onion and cook, stirring occasionally, for 5 minutes or until soft. Add the garlic and cayenne pepper and cook, stirring, for 30 seconds or until aromatic.
- Add the mushroom and tomatoes and cook, stirring occasionally, for 5 minutes or until mushroom and tomatoes soften. Add the lentils and vinegar and cook, tossing gently, for 2 minutes or until heated through. Transfer to a large heatproof bowl. Add the spinach and gently stir until just combined.
- Wipe the pan clean with paper towel. Heat the remaining oil in the pan over medium-high heat. Add the lamb and cook for 3 minutes each side for medium or until cooked to your liking. Transfer to a plate and cover with foil. Set aside for 5 minutes to rest.
- Divide the lentil salad among serving plates and top with the lamb cutlets. Serve immediately.

Nutrition Information

- Calories: 267.68 calories
- Saturated Fat: 1.5 grams saturated fat
- Total Carbohydrate: 15 grams carbohydrates
- Protein: 29 grams protein
- Total Fat: 6.5 grams fat

125. Lemon And Herb Lamb Cutlets

Serving: 0 | Prep: 15mins | Ready in: 21mins

Ingredients

- 8-10 lamb cutlets
- 1 tablespoon chopped chives
- 1/3 cup chopped mint
- 1 tablespoon lemon juice
- 1/3 cup chopped flat-leaf parsley
- 1 teaspoon finely grated lemon rind
- 1/4 cup (60ml) olive oil

Direction

- Trim cutlets of excess fat. Place oil, lemon juice, lemon rind, parsley, mint, chives and salt and pepper in a bowl. Mix well. Add cutlets and toss to coat. Cover and refrigerate for 10 minutes.
- Heat a non-stick frying pan or grill plate over medium heat. Add cutlets and cook for 3 minutes on each side or until cooked to your liking. Serve cutlets with green salad and corn on the cob.

126. Lemon And Oregano Lamb Chops

Serving: 4 | Prep: 140mins | Ready in: 190mins

Ingredients

- 12 lamb mid-loin chops, trimmed
- 800g packet frozen oven-roast onion and herb potatoes
- tzatziki dip, to serve
- 2 tablespoons olive oil
- 2 large garlic cloves, crushed
- 1 lemon, juiced
- 1 teaspoon MasterFoods® Oregano Leaves

Direction

- Make lemon and oregano marinade: Combine oil, garlic, 2 1/2 tablespoons of lemon juice and oregano in a ceramic dish.
- Add lamb to marinade and turn to coat. Cover and refrigerate for 2 hours or overnight, if time permits.
- Preheat oven to 230°C. Place potatoes in a roasting pan. Roast for 25 to 30 minutes or until golden and tender. Preheat barbecue plate on medium-high heat. Remove lamb from marinade. Barbecue lamb, basting with marinade, for 6 to 8 minutes on each side for medium or until cooked to your liking. Remove to a plate. Cover and stand for 5 minutes.
- Place lamb chops on plates. Serve with tzatziki and roast potatoes.

127. Lemon And Parsley Lamb Chops

Serving: 4 | Prep: 0S | Ready in:

Ingredients

- 2 teaspoons finely grated lemon rind
- 1 tablespoon lemon juice
- 2 tablespoons chopped fresh flat-leaf parsley leaves
- 1/4 cup olive oil
- 4 (200g each) forequarter lamb chops
- 600g nadine potatoes, quartered
- 30g butter
- 2 green onions, thinly sliced

Direction

- Combine lemon rind, lemon juice, parsley and 2 tablespoons oil in a glass or ceramic bowl. Add chops. Turn to coat. Cover and refrigerate for 2 hours.
- Cook potato in a large saucepan of boiling, salted water for 10 to 15 minutes or until just tender. Drain. Return to pan. Add butter and onions. Using a fork, lightly crush. Season with pepper. Cover.
- Meanwhile, heat remaining oil in a frying pan over medium-high heat. Remove lamb from marinade. Discard marinade. Cook for 4 to 5 minutes each side for medium or until cooked to your liking. Serve lamb with potato mixture.

Nutrition Information

- Calories: 489.233 calories
- Total Fat: 28.1 grams fat
- Saturated Fat: 10.3 grams saturated fat
- Protein: 37.7 grams protein
- Cholesterol: 125 milligrams cholesterol
- Total Carbohydrate: 19.7 grams carbohydrates
- Sodium: 156 milligrams sodium

128. Lemon And Thyme Lamb Chops

Serving: 4 | Prep: 45mins | Ready in: 57mins

Ingredients

- 4 lamb chump chops, trimmed
- 1 lemon, zested, juiced
- 1/4 cup olive oil
- 1 tablespoon Dijon mustard
- 1 tablespoon thyme, chopped
- 2 zucchini, sliced lengthways

- Salad leaves, to serve
- Lemon wedges, to serve

Direction

- Place lamb in a single layer in a shallow dish.
- In a bowl, combine lemon, oil, mustard, thyme and season to taste. Pour over lamb, turning to coat. Set aside for at least 30 mins, turning occasionally.
- Meanwhile, preheat a barbecue plate or char-grill on high. Reduce heat on medium. Cook lamb for 4-5 mins each side until cooked to taste. Rest, covered for 5 mins.
- Meanwhile, char-grill zucchini for 1-2 mins each side until tender. Serve lamb with the zucchini, salad and a lemon wedge on the side.

129. Lemon Chops With Greek Salad

Serving: 4 | Prep: 70mins | Ready in: 80mins

Ingredients

- 1 tablespoon olive oil
- 2 garlic cloves, crushed
- 1/3 cup lemon juice
- 1/4 cup chopped fresh oregano leaves
- 4 (230g each) lamb forequarter chops
- olive oil cooking spray
- 2 Lebanese cucumbers, chopped
- 100g Greek-style feta cheese, chopped
- 1/2 small red onion, thinly sliced
- 2 medium tomatoes, chopped
- 1/2 cup pitted kalamata olives
- Crusty bread, to serve
- Lemon zest, to serve

Direction

- Place oil, garlic, 2 tablespoons lemon juice and half the oregano in a glass or ceramic dish. Season with salt and pepper. Add lamb. Toss to coat. Cover and refrigerate for 1 hour.
- Spray a barbecue plate or chargrill with oil. Heat over medium-high heat. Cook lamb for 4 to 5 minutes each side for medium or until cooked to your liking.
- Meanwhile, combine cucumber, feta, onion, tomato and olives in a bowl. Season with pepper. Divide lamb and salad between plates. Top with lemon zest, remaining oregano and lemon juice. Serve with bread.

Nutrition Information

- Calories: 510.026 calories
- Total Carbohydrate: 47.8 grams carbohydrates
- Protein: 32.3 grams protein
- Cholesterol: 83 milligrams cholesterol
- Sodium: 963 milligrams sodium
- Total Fat: 19.2 grams fat
- Saturated Fat: 7.5 grams saturated fat

130. Lemon Lamb Cutlets With Cucumber Salad

Serving: 4 | Prep: 200mins | Ready in: 206mins

Ingredients

- 1/3 cup olive oil
- 1/3 cup lemon juice
- 2 tablespoons flat-leaf parsley leaves, finely chopped
- 2 tablespoons oregano leaves, chopped
- 1 garlic clove, crushed
- 12 lamb cutlets, trimmed
- 2 Lebanese cucumbers, halved lengthways, thinly sliced
- 4 tomatoes, halved, thinly sliced
- 1 small red onion, halved, thinly sliced
- 1 red capsicum, deseeded, thinly sliced

Direction

- Combine 2 tablespoons of oil, 2 tablespoons of lemon juice, parsley, oregano, garlic, and salt and pepper in a large ceramic dish. Add lamb. Turn to coat. Cover. Refrigerate for at least 3 hours.
- Preheat barbecue plate on high heat. Reduce heat to medium. Cook lamb, basting with marinade, for 3 minutes each side for medium. Remove from heat. Cover with foil. Stand for 5 minutes.
- Combine cucumber, tomatoes, onion and capsicum. Add remaining 2 tablespoons of oil, 2 tablespoons of lemon juice, and salt and pepper. Toss gently to combine.
- Serve lamb with cucumber salad.

Nutrition Information

- Calories: 492.34 calories
- Total Fat: 35 grams fat
- Saturated Fat: 9 grams saturated fat
- Total Carbohydrate: 7 grams carbohydrates
- Sugar: 7 grams sugar
- Protein: 37 grams protein
- Sodium: 137.11 milligrams sodium

131. Lemon Lamb Cutlets With Spring Vegetables

Serving: 4 | Prep: 10mins | Ready in: 35mins

Ingredients

- 1 tablespoon olive oil
- 1 tablespoon finely grated lemon rind
- 1 1/2 tablespoons lemon juice
- 12 (750g) lamb cutlets, trimmed
- 80g butter, softened
- 1 garlic clove, crushed
- 1 tablespoon finely chopped fresh mint leaves
- 1 tablespoon finely chopped fresh flat-leaf parsley leaves
- 500g chat potatoes, halved
- 200g green beans, trimmed
- 200g yellow beans, trimmed
- 150g snow peas, trimmed

Direction

- Combine oil, lemon rind and lemon juice in a shallow glass or ceramic dish. Season with salt and pepper. Add cutlets. Rub lemon mixture into cutlets.
- Combine butter, garlic, mint and parsley in a small bowl. Season with salt and pepper.
- Place potatoes in a large saucepan. Cover with cold water. Bring to the boil over high heat. Reduce heat to medium. Cook for 10 to 12 minutes or until just tender. Drain.
- Meanwhile, place beans in a metal steamer. Place steamer over a large saucepan of simmering water. Cook, covered, for 3 minutes. Add snow peas. Cook, covered, for 2 minutes or until vegetables are bright green and just tender.
- Heat a barbecue plate or chargrill on high heat. Add cutlets. Cook for 1 to 2 minutes each side for medium or until cooked to your liking. Divide cutlets and vegetables between plates. Dot vegetables with butter mixture. Serve.

Nutrition Information

- Calories: 597.261 calories
- Saturated Fat: 18 grams saturated fat
- Total Carbohydrate: 20 grams carbohydrates
- Total Fat: 37 grams fat
- Sugar: 4 grams sugar
- Protein: 42 grams protein
- Cholesterol: 171 milligrams cholesterol
- Sodium: 247.72 milligrams sodium

132. Macadamia Crumbed Lamb Cutlets With Beetroot Dip

Serving: 8 | Prep: 30mins | Ready in: 50mins

Ingredients

- 5 white bread slices, crusts removed
- 1/2 cup macadamia nuts
- 1/2 cup plain flour
- 2 eggs
- 16 lamb cutlets, french-trimmed
- 1/2 cup peanut oil
- Fresh coriander leaves, to serve
- 200g beetroot dip

Direction

- Place bread and macadamia nuts in a food processor. Process until bread forms fine breadcrumbs (macadamias should still be quite coarse). Place mixture in a shallow bowl. Season with salt and pepper. Place flour on a large plate. Lightly beat eggs in a shallow bowl.
- Using the palm of your hand gently flatten the meat on each cutlet until about 1.5cm thick. Coat 1 cutlet in flour, shaking off excess. Dip in egg. Coat in breadcrumb mixture. Place on a large baking tray lined with baking paper. Repeat with remaining cutlets, flour, egg and breadcrumb mixture. Cover. Refrigerate for 30 minutes.
- Heat half the oil in a large frying pan over medium heat. Cook cutlets in batches, adding more oil when necessary, for 3 minutes each side for medium or until cooked to your liking. Transfer to a baking tray lined with paper towel to drain.
- Place cutlets on a platter and sprinkle with coriander. Serve with beetroot dip.

Nutrition Information

- Calories: 428.049 calories
- Saturated Fat: 7 grams saturated fat
- Total Carbohydrate: 15.5 grams carbohydrates
- Cholesterol: 115 milligrams cholesterol
- Total Fat: 28.7 grams fat
- Protein: 26.9 grams protein
- Sodium: 300 milligrams sodium

133. Magic Shake And Bake Crumbed Lamb Cutlets

Serving: 4 | Prep: 20mins | Ready in: 50mins

Ingredients

- 1 2/3 cups panko breadcrumbs
- 2 teaspoons onion powder
- 1/4 cup finely chopped fresh coriander
- 2 eggs, lightly beaten
- 16 trimmed lamb cutlets
- Olive oil spray
- 150g snow peas, trimmed
- 80g baby spinach
- 1 avocado, chopped
- 1 small red onion, thinly sliced
- 150g tub roast tomato, feta, basil and cashew dip
- Extra 2 tablespoons extra virgin olive oil
- 1 tablespoon lemon juice, plus lemon wedges to serve

Direction

- Preheat oven to 180C/160C fan-forced. Line a large baking tray with baking paper.
- Combine breadcrumbs, onion powder and coriander in a large snap-lock bag. Season. Place egg and lamb in a large bowl. Toss to coat. Add lamb to breadcrumb mixture. Seal bag. Shake until lamb is well coated.
- Place on prepared tray. Spray cutlets with oil. Bake for 30 minutes or until browned and cooked through, turning halfway during cooking.
- Meanwhile, place snow peas in a medium heatproof bowl. Cover with boiling water. Stand for 2 minutes. Drain. Rinse under cold water. Drain. Thinly slice lengthways. Combine with spinach, avocado and onion.
- Combine dip, extra oil and lemon juice in a small serving bowl.
- Serve cutlets with salad, lemon wedges and dip mixture.

134. Maple Glazed Lamb Sweet Potato Tray Bake

Serving: 4 | Prep: 5mins | Ready in: 45mins

Ingredients

- 500g small sweet potatoes, scrubbed, quartered lengthways
- 12 lamb cutlets, French-trimmed
- 400g can brown lentils, rinsed, drained
- 60ml (1/4 cup) maple syrup
- 100g baby spinach

Direction

- Preheat oven to 200C/180C fan forced. Line a large shallow baking tray with baking paper. Place sweet potato on the prepared tray. Spray liberally with olive oil. Season. Bake for 20 minutes or until just tender.
- Add the lamb and lentils to the tray. Spray with oil and drizzle with maple syrup. Bake for a further 15-20 minutes or until the sweet potato is golden and lamb is cooked to your liking.
- Stir through the spinach and serve.

Nutrition Information

- Calories: 446.691 calories
- Total Fat: 11 grams fat
- Total Carbohydrate: 22 grams carbohydrates
- Protein: 26 grams protein
- Saturated Fat: 3 grams saturated fat

135. Marinated Lamb Chops

Serving: 4 | Prep: 120mins | Ready in: 158mins

Ingredients

- 1 cup (340g jar) redcurrant jelly
- 1/3 cup Massel chicken style liquid stock
- 2 tablespoons rosemary leaves
- 8 lamb loin chops
- 500g kipfler potatoes
- olive oil cooking spray
- steamed snow peas, to serve

Direction

- Combine redcurrant jelly, stock, rosemary and salt and pepper in a large, shallow ceramic dish. Add lamb and turn to coat. Cover and refrigerate for at least 2 hours, or overnight if time permits.
- Preheat oven to 200°C. Scrub potatoes clean. Cut in half lengthways and place on a tray. Spray with oil. Season with salt. Place potatoes on top shelf of oven. Roast for 30 to 35 minutes or until golden and tender.
- Preheat a barbecue plate on high heat until hot. Reduce heat to medium. Remove lamb from marinade. Reserve marinade. Barbecue lamb for 2 to 3 minutes each side for medium or until cooked to your liking.
- Pour marinade into a small saucepan over medium heat. Cook for 2 minutes or until mixture comes to the boil. Reduce heat to medium. Simmer for 2 minutes. Place chops on plates. Spoon over sauce. Serve with potatoes and snow peas.

Nutrition Information

- Calories: 597.739 calories
- Protein: 32 grams protein
- Saturated Fat: 10 grams saturated fat
- Sugar: 48 grams sugar
- Sodium: 159.77 milligrams sodium
- Total Fat: 23 grams fat
- Total Carbohydrate: 65 grams carbohydrates

136. Marinated Lamb Chops With Potato And Corn Salad

Serving: 4 | Prep: 20mins | Ready in: 35mins

Ingredients

- 4 (850g) lamb forequarter chops, trimmed
- 3 garlic cloves, unpeeled, bruised
- 2 teaspoons dried Italian herbs
- 2 tablespoons olive oil
- 1/4 cup worcestershire sauce
- 750g chat potatoes, halved
- 240g cherry truss tomatoes
- 1/3 cup whole-egg mayonnaise
- 2 teaspoons lemon juice
- 1 tablespoon dried chives
- 125g can corn kernels, drained
- Barbecue sauce, to serve

Direction

- At home Place chops in a large snap-lock bag. Add garlic, Italian herbs, oil and Worcestershire sauce. Seal bag, removing as much air as possible. Freeze.
- Place potatoes in a large saucepan. Cover with cold water. Bring to the boil over high heat. Reduce heat to medium. Cook for 10 to 12 minutes or until just tender. Drain.
- Meanwhile, heat a barbecue plate or chargrill over medium-high heat. Cook chops for 3 to 4 minutes each side for medium or until cooked to your liking. Transfer to a plate. Cover with foil. Stand for 5 minutes. Meanwhile, add tomatoes to barbecue or chargrill. Cook for 4 to 5 minutes or until starting to collapse.
- Combine mayonnaise, lemon juice and chives in a bowl. Add potatoes and corn. Toss to combine. Serve chops with tomatoes, potato salad and barbecue sauce.

Nutrition Information

- Calories: 572.883 calories
- Total Fat: 31.4 grams fat
- Total Carbohydrate: 44 grams carbohydrates
- Protein: 25.7 grams protein
- Cholesterol: 89 milligrams cholesterol
- Saturated Fat: 5.8 grams saturated fat
- Sodium: 546 milligrams sodium

137. Massaman Lamb Cutlets With Crunchy Coconut Potatoes

Serving: 4 | Prep: 25mins | Ready in: 60mins

Ingredients

- 1/4 cup (75g) Massaman curry paste
- 1/2 cup (125ml) coconut cream
- 1/3 cup (30g) desiccated coconut, toasted
- 2/3 cup (100g) finely ground roasted peanuts
- 12 French-trimmed lamb cutlets
- 1/2 teaspoon ground coriander
- 1/2 teaspoon ground cumin
- 1/3 cup (80ml) sunflower oil
- 1kg King Edward or sebago potatoes, cut into 2cm pieces, blanched
- Coriander leaves, to serve
- Lime wedges, to serve
- Natural yoghurt, to serve

Direction

- Preheat the oven to 200°C and line a baking tray with foil.
- Combine curry paste, coconut cream, 2 tablespoons desiccated coconut and half the peanuts in a bowl. Coat the cutlets in the mixture and marinate for 15 minutes.
- Meanwhile, place the spices and 1/4 cup (60ml) oil in a saucepan over medium heat for 3 minutes or until the oil is hot and fragrant. Scatter the potato on the tray, then pour over the oil and season. Roast for 20-25 minutes until golden and crisp. Toss potato with the remaining 2 tablespoons coconut and 1/3 cup (50g) peanuts.
- While the potatoes are roasting, heat the remaining 1 tablespoon oil in a large fry pan. Season lamb, then in batches, cook for 2-3

minutes each side for medium-rare. Rest for 5 minutes. Serve with potatoes, coriander leaves, lime and yoghurt.

Nutrition Information

- Calories: 910.112 calories
- Total Fat: 60 grams fat
- Total Carbohydrate: 43 grams carbohydrates
- Sugar: 11 grams sugar
- Sodium: 830.4 milligrams sodium
- Protein: 47 grams protein
- Cholesterol: 121 milligrams cholesterol
- Saturated Fat: 21 grams saturated fat

138. Meatlovers' Platter Recipe

Serving: 6 | Prep: 50mins | Ready in: 105mins

Ingredients

- Crusty sourdough bread, sliced
- 60ml (1/4 cup) olive oil
- 1 tablespoon Portuguese chicken seasoning
- 2 garlic cloves, crushed
- 1 lemon, rind finely grated, juiced
- 750g chicken wing nibbles, trimmed
- 1 bunch fresh continental parsley, leaves picked
- 1/2 bunch fresh coriander, leaves picked
- 1 bunch fresh chives, chopped
- 2 garlic cloves, crushed
- 3 teaspoons red wine vinegar
- 1/2 teaspoon chilli flakes
- 80ml (1/3 cup) extra virgin olive oil
- 8 lamb cutlets, frenched

Direction

- For the Spicy Portuguese chicken nibbles, preheat the oven to 200C/180C fan forced. Grease a baking tray and line with baking paper. Combine the oil, Portuguese seasoning, garlic, lemon rind and 1 tbsp. juice in a glass or ceramic dish. Season. Add the chicken and toss to coat. Set aside for 30 minutes to marinate.
- Arrange chicken in a single layer on the prepared tray. Bake for 30-40 minutes, turning occasionally, until chicken is cooked.
- To make the chimichurri, process parsley, coriander, chives, garlic, vinegar and chilli flakes until finely chopped. Gradually add olive oil until well combined. Season well.
- Season lamb. Heat a barbecue or chargrill plate over medium-high heat. Spray with oil. Cook lamb for 2-3 minutes each side for medium rare. Transfer to a plate, cover and rest for 5 minutes before serving with sauce.

139. Mediterranean Barbecued Lamb Chops

Serving: 4 | Prep: 10mins | Ready in: 20mins

Ingredients

- 1/4 cup Mediterranean-style herb paste
- 1 tablespoon olive oil
- 12 Coles Australian Lamb Loin Chops
- 400g Coles Bakery Turkish Bread, cut into 3cm slices
- 2 x 300g Coles Australian Mediterranean Style Salad bowls
- 1/3 cup (80ml) balsamic dressing
- 60g fetta, crumbled
- Lemon wedges, to serve

Direction

- Combine the herb paste and oil in a small bowl. Heat a barbecue or chargrill plate on medium-high heat. Cook the lamb, brushing with the oil mixture, for 3 mins each side or until cooked to your liking. Transfer to a plate. Cover with foil and set aside for 5 mins to rest.

- Meanwhile, cook the bread on the same barbecue or chargrill plate, turning, for 3 mins or until browned all over.
- Toss the salad contents with the balsamic dressing. Divide the salad mixture, lamb and bread among serving plates. Sprinkle with feta. Serve with lemon wedges.

140. Minted Lamb Chops With Hot Potato Salad

Serving: 4 | Prep: 15mins | Ready in: 25mins

Ingredients

- 8 (about 800g) lamb chops
- 2 garlic cloves, crushed
- 2 tablespoons malt vinegar
- 1 tablespoon olive oil
- 2 teaspoons raw sugar
- 2 tablespoons coarsely chopped mint
- 2 teaspoons coarsely chopped rosemary
- Steamed peas, to serve
- 500g baby coliban (chat) potatoes
- 1/3 cup (80g) good-quality whole-egg mayonnaise
- 2 tablespoons sour cream
- 4 green onions, trimmed, thinly sliced
- 2 tablespoons finely shredded mint
- 1 tablespoon green peppercorns, coarsely chopped
- 1/4 cup finely chopped chives

Direction

- Place the lamb chops in a glass or ceramic dish. Combine the garlic, vinegar, oil, sugar, mint and rosemary in a jug. Pour evenly over the lamb and turn to coat. Set aside for 15 minutes to marinate.
- To make the salad, place potatoes in a medium saucepan and cover with cold water. Place over high heat; bring to the boil. Cook for 10 minutes or until tender. Drain well. Combine mayonnaise, sour cream, green onions, mint, peppercorns and half the chives in a bowl. Pour over the potatoes and gently toss to combine.
- Meanwhile, heat a char-grill pan over high heat. Add lamb and cook for 3 minutes each side for medium or until cooked to your liking. Transfer to a plate and cover with foil. Set aside for 5 minutes to rest.
- Spoon the potato salad among serving plates and sprinkle with chives. Serve with lamb and steamed peas, if desired.

Nutrition Information

- Calories: 696.924 calories
- Total Carbohydrate: 27 grams carbohydrates
- Protein: 43 grams protein
- Cholesterol: 130 milligrams cholesterol
- Total Fat: 45 grams fat
- Saturated Fat: 17 grams saturated fat
- Sugar: 11 grams sugar
- Sodium: 252.63 milligrams sodium

141. Minted Lamb Cutlets

Serving: 4 | Prep: 5mins | Ready in: 15mins

Ingredients

- 12 French-trimmed lamb cutlets
- 1 1/2 cups firmly-packed mint leaves
- 1/2 cup slivered almonds
- 2 garlic cloves, roughly chopped
- 1/2 cup extra-virgin olive oil
- 60g parmesan cheese, finely grated

Direction

- Make pesto: Place mint, almonds and garlic in a food processor. Process (scraping down sides occasionally) until almost smooth. With the motor running, add oil in a slow and steady stream. Process until all oil is combined. Transfer pesto to a bowl. Add parmesan.

Season with salt and pepper. Stir until well combined.
- Preheat a grill on medium-high heat. Place a wire rack over a large baking tray.
- Place cutlets on wire rack. Spread 1 teaspoon pesto over each cutlet.
- Place cutlets under grill and cook for 3 minutes. Turn cutlets over and spread 1 teaspoon pesto over uncooked side. Grill for a further 3 to 4 minutes for medium or until cooked to your liking.

Nutrition Information

- Calories: 511.699 calories
- Total Fat: 38 grams fat
- Saturated Fat: 10 grams saturated fat
- Total Carbohydrate: 5 grams carbohydrates
- Sugar: 1 grams sugar
- Protein: 37 grams protein
- Sodium: 877.84 milligrams sodium

142. Minty Lamb Chops With Vegetable Crumble

Serving: 4 | Prep: 25mins | Ready in: 75mins

Ingredients

- 500g orange sweet potato, peeled, cut into 2cm dice
- 2 parsnips, peeled, cut into 2cm dice
- 2 carrots, peeled, cut into 2cm dice
- 30g butter
- 1/4 cup plain flour
- 1/2 cup thickened cream
- 1 1/2 cups fresh breadcrumbs
- 1 cup grated tasty cheese
- 8 (800g) lamb chump chops
- 2 tablespoons Fountain Thick Mint Sauce
- Olive oil cooking spray
- Extra mint sauce, to serve

Direction

- Lightly grease a 1.5L-capacity baking dish. Place potato, parsnip and carrot in a medium saucepan. Cover with cold water. Bring to the boil over high heat. Cook for 12 to 15 minutes until tender. Drain, reserving 2 cups cooking liquid. Transfer vegetables to prepared dish.
- Preheat oven to 180°C/160°C fan-forced. Melt butter in a medium saucepan over medium heat. Add flour. Cook, stirring, for 2 minutes. Gradually add reserved cooking liquid and cream. Cook, stirring, for 5 minutes or until mixture thickens. Season with salt and pepper. Pour over vegetables.
- Combine breadcrumbs and cheese. Sprinkle over vegetables. Bake for 40 minutes or until golden. Set aside for 10 minutes to stand.
- Place chops in a glass or ceramic baking dish. Add sauce. Toss to coat. Stand for 15 minutes. Lightly spray a chargrill pan with oil. Place pan over medium-high heat. Season chops with salt and pepper. Cook chops, in batches, for 3 to 4 minutes each side or until cooked to your liking. Transfer to a plate. Serve with crumble and extra sauce.

Nutrition Information

- Calories: 812.361 calories
- Cholesterol: 176 milligrams cholesterol
- Sodium: 533.66 milligrams sodium
- Sugar: 15 grams sugar
- Total Fat: 46 grams fat
- Saturated Fat: 25 grams saturated fat
- Total Carbohydrate: 48 grams carbohydrates
- Protein: 49 grams protein

143. Minty Lamb With Beetroot And Charred Broccoli

Serving: 4 | Prep: 20mins | Ready in: 35mins

Ingredients

- 1/2 bunch mint, leaves chopped

- 1/2 bunch flat-leaf parsley, leaves chopped
- 1/4 cup (40g) pine nuts, toasted
- 2 tablespoons parmesan, grated
- 1 garlic clove, finely chopped
- 2/3 cup (165ml) olive oil, plus extra to brush
- 12 x French-trimmed lamb cutlets
- 3 teaspoons dried mint
- 1 broccoli, sliced lengthways
- 1 1/2 tablespoons lemon juice
- 100g watercress
- 2 beetroots, cut into thin matchsticks
- 120g marinated feta, drained, crumbled

Direction

- Whiz the fresh mint, parsley, pine nuts, parmesan and garlic in a food processor until a paste. Gradually add 1/2 cup (125ml) oil and whiz until combined. Set aside.
- Brush lamb with a little extra oil, then season and coat in dried mint. In a separate bowl, toss broccoli and 1 tbsp. oil. Preheat a chargrill pan to medium-high heat. Cook broccoli, turning, for 3-4 minutes until lightly charred. Set aside. Cook lamb for 4 minutes each side for medium-rare or until cooked to your liking.
- Whisk the lemon juice and remaining 1 tbsp. oil together in a bowl. Season.
- Arrange broccoli, watercress, beetroot and feta on a platter. Top with the lamb, then drizzle over lemon dressing and mint pesto to serve.

144. Mongolian Lamb Chops With Asian Greens

Serving: 4 | Prep: 15mins | Ready in: 25mins

Ingredients

- 1 tablespoon hoisin sauce
- 2 tablespoons mirin
- 2 garlic cloves, crushed
- 1 tablespoon soy sauce
- 4 x 200g Coles Australian lamb forequarter chops
- 1 tablespoon peanut oil
- 2 red onions, cut into wedges
- 1 spring onion, cut into strips
- 1 long red chilli, cut into strips
- 1 teaspoon sesame seeds
- 2 bunches baby buk choy, trimmed, halved lengthways, steamed
- Steamed jasmine rice, to serve

Direction

- Combine hoisin, mirin, garlic and soy sauce in a bowl. Add lamb and turn to coat. Marinate for 1 hour, if time permits.
- Heat oil in a large frying pan on medium heat. Cook lamb for 3 mins each side or until cooked to your liking, reserving marinade. Transfer to a plate. Cover to keep warm.
- Add red onion to pan. Cook, stirring, for 3 mins or until softened. Add reserved marinade. Cook, stirring, to combine. Divide lamb among plates and top with red onion, spring onion, chili and sesame seeds. Serve with bok choy and steamed rice.

145. Mongolian Lamb Chops With Rice Salad

Serving: 4 | Prep: 15mins | Ready in: 25mins

Ingredients

- 1/4 cup soy sauce
- 2 tablespoons black bean sauce
- 1 tablespoon brown sugar
- 1/4 cup rice vinegar
- 2 garlic cloves, crushed
- 8 x 100g lamb chump chops
- 2 teaspoons cornflour
- 3 cups cooked jasmine rice (see note)
- 100g snow peas, trimmed, thinly sliced
- 1 1/2 cups bean sprouts
- 3 green onions, thinly sliced
- 1 small red capsicum, thinly sliced
- 1 tablespoon sesame oil

- Extra sliced green onions, to serve

Direction

- Combine sauces, sugar, half the vinegar and half the garlic in a large shallow glass or ceramic dish. Add lamb. Turn to coat. Refrigerate for 1 hour.
- Heat a chargrill or barbecue plate on medium-high heat. Drain lamb, reserving marinade. Cook lamb for 3 to 4 minutes each side or until cooked to your liking. Transfer to a plate. Cover loosely with foil. Set aside for 5 minutes.
- Meanwhile, place reserved marinade in a small saucepan over medium heat. Bring to the boil. Blend cornflour in a small jug with 2 teaspoons cold water. Stir cornflour mixture into marinade. Cook, stirring, until sauce thickens slightly. Remove from heat. Cover.
- Combine rice, snow peas, sprouts, onion and capsicum in a medium bowl. Place oil, vinegar and remaining garlic in a small bowl. Whisk until well combined. Season with salt and pepper. Add dressing to salad. Toss gently to combine. Drizzle lamb with sauce. Sprinkle with extra green onions. Serve with rice salad.

Nutrition Information

- Calories: 633.35 calories
- Cholesterol: 131 milligrams cholesterol
- Sodium: 1634.58 milligrams sodium
- Total Fat: 27 grams fat
- Saturated Fat: 9 grams saturated fat
- Total Carbohydrate: 47 grams carbohydrates
- Protein: 49 grams protein
- Sugar: 8 grams sugar

146. Moroccan Lamb Chops With Quinoa Salad

Serving: 4 | Prep: 30mins | Ready in: 55mins

Ingredients

- 1 cup (200g) quinoa, rinsed
- 1/3 cup (80ml) olive oil
- 2 tablespoons lemon juice
- 1 clove garlic, crushed
- 1 tablespoon Moroccan seasoning
- Salt and pepper
- 4 Coles Australian Lamb Forequarter Chops
- 3 spring onions, finely chopped
- 400g can Coles Brand Chickpeas, drained, rinsed
- 1/2 cup Always Fresh Marinated Fire Roasted Red Peppers Strips
- 1 cup mint leaves
- 1 cup parsley leaves
- 100g fetta, crumbled
- 2 tablespoons pine nuts, toasted

Direction

- Cook quinoa following packet directions. Drain. Rinse under cold running water. Transfer to a bowl.
- Meanwhile, combine 2 tablespoons olive oil, 2 tablespoons lemon juice, garlic and Moroccan seasoning in a shallow glass or ceramic dish. Season with salt and pepper. Add lamb chops and turn to coat. Set aside to marinate for 10 minutes.
- Spray a barbecue grill or char-grill pan with olive oil spray. Heat over medium-high heat. Add the lamb and cook for 2-3 mins each side for medium or until cooked to your liking. Transfer to a plate and set aside for 5 mins to rest.
- Add onion, chickpeas, capsicum, mint, parsley, feta and pine nuts to the quinoa. Combine remaining olive oil and lemon juice in a small bowl and pour over salad. Season with salt and pepper and toss to combine. Divide the salad and lamb chops among serving plates.

147. Moroccan Lamb Cutlets With Cauliflower Pilaf

Serving: 4 | Prep: 15mins | Ready in: 30mins

Ingredients

- 12 Coles Australian Lamb Cutlets
- 2 tablespoons olive oil
- 1 tablespoon Moroccan seasoning
- 400g can chickpeas, rinsed, drained
- 1 red onion, thinly sliced
- 1 garlic clove, crushed
- 300g pkt Coles Australian Cauliflower Rice (see notes)
- 1 lemon, zested, juiced
- 1/2 cup chopped coriander
- Lemon wedges, to serve

Direction

- Place the lamb, half the oil and Moroccan seasoning in a shallow ceramic dish. Turn to coat lamb. Season well.
- Heat a barbecue grill or chargrill on medium-high. Cook the lamb for 3 mins each side or until cooked to your liking. Transfer to a plate. Cover with foil and set aside for 5 mins to rest.
- Meanwhile, heat the remaining oil in a large frying pan over high heat. Add the chickpeas, onion and garlic and cook, stirring occasionally, for 4 mins or until onion is soft and chickpeas are golden. Add the cauliflower rice and cook, stirring, for 5 mins or until cauliflower is tender. Stir in the lemon juice and coriander.
- Divide the cauliflower pilaf among serving plates. Top with lamb and sprinkle with lemon zest. Serve with the lemon wedges.

148. Moroccan Lamb Loin Chops With Mango Couscous

Serving: 4 | Prep: 15mins | Ready in: 25mins

Ingredients

- 1 cup couscous
- 1 red capsicum, diced
- 1 shallot, finely chopped
- 1 mango, flesh diced
- 1/4 cup currants
- 1/4 cup slivered almonds
- 1/3 cup chopped fresh mint
- 2/3 cup natural Greek yoghurt
- 1 tablespoon Gourmet Garden Moroccan stir-in seasoning
- 4 x 150g Coles lamb loin chops
- 1 teaspoon olive oil

Direction

- Place the couscous in a large heatproof bowl. Stir in 1 cup boiling water. Cover and set aside for 5 minutes to soak. Use a fork to separate the grains. Add the capsicum, shallot, mango, currants, almond and mint. Season with salt and pepper. Mix until well combined.
- Combine the yoghurt and 1 teaspoon of the seasoning in a small bowl. Season with salt and pepper.
- Spread the remaining paste over both sides of the chops. Heat the oil in a large non-stick frying pan over medium heat. Cook the chops for 3 minutes each side or until golden.
- Divide the chops, couscous and yoghurt among serving plates.

Nutrition Information

- Calories: 587.223 calories
- Total Fat: 17.4 grams fat
- Sugar: 10.5 grams sugar
- Total Carbohydrate: 52.4 grams carbohydrates
- Protein: 52.8 grams protein
- Cholesterol: 135 milligrams cholesterol
- Sodium: 517 milligrams sodium
- Saturated Fat: 4.5 grams saturated fat

149. Moroccan Lamb With Bean Puree

Serving: 4 | Prep: 10mins | Ready in: 35mins

Ingredients

- 47g jar Moroccan seasoning
- 2 tablespoons plain flour
- 12 to 16 lamb cutlets, trimmed
- 500g baby trussed tomatoes
- 1/4 cup olive oil
- 2 x 400g cans butter beans, rinsed and drained
- Zest and juice of 2 small lemons

Direction

- Preheat oven to 200°C.
- Combine Moroccan seasoning and flour in a plastic bag. Add cutlets, one at a time, and shake until well-coated. Place cutlets into a large baking dish.
- Place dish onto the oven's top shelf and bake for 8 minutes.
- Place tomatoes onto a lined baking tray. Drizzle with 1 tablespoon olive oil. Place under cutlets in oven. Bake for 15 to 20 minutes.
- Pulse beans, lemon rind and juice, and remaining oil in a food processor until smooth. Serve with cutlets and tomatoes.

Nutrition Information

- Calories: 599.89 calories
- Cholesterol: 161 milligrams cholesterol
- Sodium: 1261.84 milligrams sodium
- Total Fat: 36 grams fat
- Saturated Fat: 11 grams saturated fat
- Total Carbohydrate: 16 grams carbohydrates
- Sugar: 8 grams sugar
- Protein: 51 grams protein

150. Moroccan Lamb With Carrot And Radish Salad

Serving: 0 | Prep: 15mins | Ready in: 25mins

Ingredients

- 2 tablespoons extra virgin olive oil
- 4 Coles Australian Lamb Forequarter Chops
- 2 tablespoons Moroccan herb paste
- 2 tablespoons lemon juice
- 1/2 teaspoon ground cumin
- 4 carrots, peeled into ribbons
- 1 bunch radishes, trimmed, thinly sliced
- 1/2 cup mint leaves
- 1/2 cup (140g) Greek-style yoghurt
- 2 teaspoons lemon rind, grated

Direction

- Heat 1 tablespoon of oil in a large frying pan over medium-high heat. Add the lamb and cook for 2 mins each side or until browned. Brush both sides of lamb with herb paste. Cook for a further 1 min each side. Transfer to a plate and cover with foil. Set aside for 5 mins to rest.
- Meanwhile, combine lemon juice, cumin and remaining oil in a large bowl. Season. Add carrot, radish and mint and toss to combine.
- Divide salad among serving plates. Top with lamb. Serve with yoghurt and sprinkle with lemon rind.

151. Moroccan Spiced Lamb Chops With Moghrabieh And Roasted Beetroot

Serving: 4 | Prep: 10mins | Ready in: 60mins

Ingredients

- 2 bunches baby beetroot (red and gold), trimmed

- 2 cups (450g) moghrabieh (large pearl couscous - see notes)
- 8 lamb loin chops
- 1/2 tsp ground cumin
- 1/2 tsp ground cinnamon
- 3 tsp zaatar (see notes)
- 1/3 cup (80ml) olive oil
- 1 tbs red wine vinegar
- 1/2 bunch mint, leaves picked
- 1/4 cup (35g) slivered almonds, toasted
- Thick Greek-style yoghurt, to serve

Direction

- Preheat the oven to 200C. Wrap each beetroot in foil and place on a baking tray. Roast for 35-40 minutes until tender.
- Meanwhile, cook the moghrabieh according to the packet instructions.
- Season lamb with cumin, cinnamon, salt and pepper, and 1 tsp. za'atar. Heat 2 tbsp. oil in a fry pan over medium-high heat and cook lamb, turning, for 6-8 minutes for medium or until cooked to your liking.
- Set aside, loosely covered with foil, for 5 minutes to rest.
- Add remaining 2 tbsp. olive oil to the moghrabieh with vinegar and remaining 2 tsp. za'atar. Unwrap the beetroot, rub off the skins and halve. Serve lamb with moghrabieh, mint, almonds and yoghurt.

Nutrition Information

- Calories: 981.812 calories
- Protein: 65 grams protein
- Saturated Fat: 7.5 grams saturated fat
- Total Carbohydrate: 99.4 grams carbohydrates
- Sugar: 7.2 grams sugar
- Cholesterol: 153 milligrams cholesterol
- Sodium: 204 milligrams sodium
- Total Fat: 37.4 grams fat

152. Moroccan Spiced Lamb Cutlets With Lentil Chickpea Salad

Serving: 4 | Prep: 20mins | Ready in: 45mins

Ingredients

- 1 cup dried whole green lentils
- 1 teaspoon ground cumin
- 1 teaspoon sweet paprika
- 1/2 teaspoon ground allspice
- 1/2 teaspoon ground cardamom
- 1/2 teaspoon ground cayenne pepper
- 1/2 teaspoon ground cinnamon
- 1/2 teaspoon ground ginger
- 12 Coles Australian lamb cutlets, frenched or trimmed
- 2 tbsp olive oil, plus 1/4 cup extra-virgin olive oil
- 400g can chickpeas, drained, rinsed, patted dry
- 1 celery stalk, cut into 1.5cm dice
- 1 medium carrot, peeled, cut into 1.5cm dice
- 1/2 medium red capsicum, cut into 1.5cm dice
- 2/3 cup thinly sliced spring onions (about 6)
- 1/2 cup fresh mint leaves, lightly packed, finely chopped
- 1/2 cup flat-leaf parsley leaves, lightly packed, finely chopped
- 1 clove garlic, crushed
- 1 teaspoon lemon zest, grated finely
- 1/3 cup fresh lemon juice
- Mixed lettuce, for serving

Direction

- In a large saucepan, bring 3 cups of water to a boil over high heat. Add the lentils. Reduce the heat to medium-low, cover, and simmer for about 25 minutes, or until the lentils are just tender. Drain well. Arrange the lentils over large baking tray to cool completely.
- In a small bowl, mix all the dry spices together. Place the cutlets on a baking tray and coat with 2 tablespoons of the oil. Coat both sides of the cutlets with the spice mixture. Set

aside to marinate while you prepare the barbecue for medium-high heat.
- In a large bowl, toss the lentils, chickpeas, celery, carrot, capsicum, spring onions, mint, parsley, garlic, and lemon zest. Add the lemon juice and remaining 1/4 cup oil and toss to coat. Season the salad to taste with salt and pepper.
- Barbecue the cutlets for about 3 minutes per side, or until nicely charred on the outside and the internal temperature of the cutlets is 50C for medium-rare doneness. Set the cutlets aside to rest for 3 minutes. Arrange the mixed greens on a platter and spoon the lentil salad over. Serve with the cutlets.

has softened. Add seasoning. Cook, stirring, for 1 minute or until fragrant.
- Return chops to dish. Add tomato, chickpeas, carrot and stock. Stir to combine. Season with pepper. Cover tightly with foil. Bake for 2 hours or until lamb is tender. Remove foil. Bake for 30 minutes or until sauce has reduced slightly.
- Sprinkle with parsley. Serve with couscous.

Nutrition Information

- Calories: 761.932 calories
- Total Carbohydrate: 16 grams carbohydrates
- Total Fat: 55 grams fat
- Saturated Fat: 15 grams saturated fat
- Sodium: 526.52 milligrams sodium
- Sugar: 7 grams sugar
- Protein: 48 grams protein
- Cholesterol: 146 milligrams cholesterol

153. Moroccan Style Lamb Chops

Serving: 4 | Prep: 10mins | Ready in: 175mins

Ingredients

- 1 tablespoon olive oil
- 8 (1.2kg) small lamb forequarter or shoulder chops, trimmed
- 1 large brown onion, cut into wedges
- 2 garlic cloves, crushed
- 1 tablespoon Moroccan seasoning
- 400g can crushed tomatoes
- 400g can chickpeas, drained, rinsed
- 2 medium carrots, peeled, cut into 1cm slices
- 1/2 cup Massel chicken style liquid stock
- 1 tablespoon chopped fresh flat-leaf parsley leaves
- Couscous, to serve

Direction

- Preheat oven to 160°C/140°C fan-forced. Heat oil in a 10 cup-capacity flameproof, ovenproof dish over high heat. Cook lamb, in batches, for 2 to 3 minutes each side or until just browned. Transfer to a plate. Add onion and garlic to dish. Cook for 2 to 3 minutes or until onion

154. Mustard Lamb Cutlets With Mint Aioli And Char Grilled Potatoes

Serving: 4 | Prep: 10mins | Ready in: 30mins

Ingredients

- 12 (about 1.2kg) lamb cutlets
- 1 tablespoon wholegrain mustard
- 2 garlic cloves, crushed
- 2 tablespoons olive oil
- 250g kipfler potatoes, sliced diagonally
- 200g snow peas
- 1 bunch asparagus, trimmed, halved
- 1/4 cup mint leaves
- 1 garlic clove, crushed
- 1 egg yolk
- 1/2 teaspoon mustard powder
- 1 tablespoon malt or cider vinegar
- 1/2 cup (125ml) light olive oil

Direction

- Combine the lamb, mustard, garlic and 2 teaspoonfuls of the oil in a medium bowl. Set aside for 15 minutes to marinate.
- Meanwhile, cook the potatoes in a saucepan of boiling water for 7-8 minutes or until almost tender. Add the snow peas and cook for a further 1 minute or until tender crisp. Refresh under cold running water.
- To make the mint aioli, place the mint, garlic, egg yolk, mustard powder and vinegar in the bowl of a food processor and process until combined. With the motor running, gradually add the oil in a thin, steady stream until mixture is thick and pale. Season with salt and pepper.
- Preheat a barbecue or char-grill pan on high. Add the lamb to the grill and cook for 2 minutes each side for medium or until cooked to your liking. Transfer to a plate and cover with foil. Set aside for 5 minutes to rest. Brush the potatoes and asparagus with remaining oil. Add the potatoes to the grill and cook for 2 minutes each side or until charred. Add the asparagus and cook for 2 minutes or until just tender. Remove from heat.
- Arrange the potato, snow peas and asparagus on serving plates. Top with lamb and dollop with aioli.

Nutrition Information

- Calories: 881.671 calories
- Total Carbohydrate: 11 grams carbohydrates
- Sugar: 3 grams sugar
- Saturated Fat: 17 grams saturated fat
- Total Fat: 65 grams fat
- Protein: 62 grams protein
- Sodium: 270.62 milligrams sodium

155. Orange Chilli Lamb Cutlets With Warm White Bean Salad

Serving: 4 | Prep: 10mins | Ready in: 30mins

Ingredients

- 12 (about 720g) lamb cutlets, French trimmed
- 1 orange, rind finely grated, juiced
- 1 long red fresh chilli, finely chopped
- 1 teaspoon ground cumin
- 1 tablespoon balsamic vinegar
- 1 tablespoon extra virgin olive oil
- 1 small red onion, finely chopped
- 2 garlic cloves, crushed
- 65g (1/3 cup) raisins
- 125g (1/2 cup) drained roasted red capsicum, finely chopped
- 40g (1/4 cup) pitted kalamata olives, halved
- 2 x 400g cans cannellini beans, rinsed, drained
- 1 cup fresh continental parsley, chopped
- 90g (1/3 cup) Tamar Valley Greek Style Yoghurt, to serve, optional
- Extra virgin olive oil for drizzling

Direction

- Combine the lamb cutlets, orange rind, half the orange juice, chilli and cumin in a bowl. Set aside to marinate for 10 minutes. Combine remaining orange juice and vinegar in a small bowl. Set aside.
- Meanwhile, to make the bean salad, heat the oil in a large non-stick frying pan over medium heat. Cook onion, stirring, for 3 minutes or until soft. Stir in garlic and raisins for 2 minutes or until aromatic. Stir in capsicum and olives for 2 minutes or until warmed through. Stir in cannellini beans for 3 minutes or until warmed through. Remove from heat. Stir in parsley. Season. Keep warm.
- Drain excess marinade from lamb. Season. Heat a large frying pan over medium-high heat. Spray with olive oil. Cook lamb, in 2 batches, for 4 minutes, turning, for medium or until cooked to your liking. Return all lamb

cutlets to pan and pour over orange and balsamic mixture. Simmer for 1 minute or until reduced slightly.
- Divide bean mixture among serving plates. Top with lamb cutlets and drizzle with pan juices and extra virgin olive oil. Serve with the yoghurt.

156. Oregano And Lemon Lamb Chops With Greek Salad

Serving: 4 | Prep: 25mins | Ready in: 35mins

Ingredients

- 1/3 cup (80ml) olive oil
- 1 garlic clove, crushed
- 1/4 cup (60ml) lemon juice
- 1/4 cup finely chopped oregano leaves
- 1 tablespoon finely grated lemon rind
- 6 Coles Australian Lamb Forequarter Chops
- 1 tablespoon white wine vinegar
- 400g mixed baby tomatoes, halved
- 2 Lebanese cucumbers, coarsely chopped
- 1/2 red onion, thinly sliced
- 1 small red capsicum, coarsely chopped
- 80g baby spinach leaves
- 1/2 cup (75g) pitted Kalamata olives
- 200g feta, coarsely chopped

Direction

- Combine the oil, garlic, lemon juice and oregano in a shallow glass or ceramic dish. Divide into 2 even portions. Add the lemon rind to 1 portion and place in a large glass or ceramic dish. Add lamb chops and turn to coat. Add vinegar to remaining lemon mixture and set aside
- Spray a barbecue plate or chargrill pan with olive oil spray. Heat over medium-high heat. Cook lamb for 2-3 mins each side for medium or until cooked to your liking. Set aside for 5 mins to rest.

- Meanwhile combine the tomato, cucumber, onion, capsicum, spinach, olives, and feta in a large bowl. Drizzle with remaining lemon mixture and toss to combine. Divide Greek salad and lamb among serving plates to serve.

157. Peppered Lamb Chops With Rhubarb And Fetta Couscous

Serving: 4 | Prep: 15mins | Ready in: 30mins

Ingredients

- 4 rhubarb stalks, trimmed, cut into 5cm lengths
- Olive oil cooking spray
- 2 teaspoons honey
- 8 lamb loin chops (see notes)
- 1 teaspoon finely ground peppercorn medley (see notes)
- 2 tablespoons extra virgin olive oil
- 1 1/2 cups couscous
- 1 1/2 cups boiling water
- 1/2 red onion, finely chopped
- 1/2 cup fresh mint leaves, roughly torn
- 1/2 cup chopped fresh coriander leaves
- 100g feta, crumbled
- 2 tablespoons lemon juice

Direction

- Preheat oven to 200C/180C fan-forced. Line a baking tray with baking paper. Place rhubarb on prepared tray. Lightly spray with oil. Drizzle with honey. Roast for 12 to 15 minutes or until tender.
- Meanwhile, sprinkle chops with ground peppercorns. Heat ½ the oil in a large frying pan over medium-high heat. Cook chops for 3 to 4 minutes each side for medium or until cooked to your liking.
- Place couscous in a heatproof bowl. Pour over boiling water. Cover. Set aside for 5 minutes or

until water has absorbed. Fluff couscous with a fork to separate grains.
- Add onion, mint, coriander, feta, lemon juice, roasted rhubarb and remaining oil to couscous. Gently toss to combine. Serve couscous with lamb chops.

Nutrition Information

- Calories: 732.774 calories
- Saturated Fat: 12 grams saturated fat
- Sodium: 472 milligrams sodium
- Total Fat: 30.9 grams fat
- Total Carbohydrate: 51.8 grams carbohydrates
- Protein: 58.5 grams protein
- Cholesterol: 141 milligrams cholesterol

158. Pesto Lamb Chops With Risoni Salad

Serving: 4 | Prep: 15mins | Ready in: 40mins

Ingredients

- 1 cup dried risoni pasta
- 2 tablespoons olive oil
- 4 (185g each) lamb forequarter chops
- 1/3 cup sun-dried tomato pesto
- 2 small zucchini, thinly sliced
- 250g cherry tomatoes, halved
- 1 small red onion, halved, thinly sliced
- 2 tablespoons red wine vinegar

Direction

- Cook pasta in a saucepan of boiling, salted water, following packet directions, until tender. Drain. Place in a large bowl. Add half the oil. Toss to combine.
- Place chops on a plate. Spread 1 teaspoon pesto over each side of chops. Place zucchini, tomato and remaining oil in a bowl. Toss to coat. Heat a greased barbecue plate or chargrill over medium-high heat. Cook vegetables for 2 to 3 minutes or until golden and tender. Add to pasta with onion and vinegar.
- Cook chops for 4 to 5 minutes each side for medium or until cooked to your liking. Dollop with remaining pesto. Serve with pasta mixture.

Nutrition Information

- Calories: 711.264 calories
- Saturated Fat: 10 grams saturated fat
- Total Carbohydrate: 44 grams carbohydrates
- Sugar: 6 grams sugar
- Cholesterol: 90 milligrams cholesterol
- Total Fat: 43 grams fat
- Protein: 35 grams protein
- Sodium: 347.61 milligrams sodium

159. Pita Cucumber Salad With Dukkah Lamb Cutlets

Serving: 4 | Prep: 20mins | Ready in: 30mins

Ingredients

- 1 piece wholemeal Lebanese bread
- Olive oil spray
- 8 lamb cutlets, French trimmed
- 1 tablespoon almond dukkah
- 2 Lebanese cucumbers, coarsely chopped
- 1 large red capsicum, halved, deseeded, coarsely chopped
- 4 shallots, ends trimmed, thinly sliced
- 2 tablespoons chopped fresh continental parsley
- 2 tablespoons chopped fresh mint leaves
- 1 tablespoon fresh lemon juice

Direction

- Preheat oven to 200°C. Place the bread on a large baking tray. Bake in oven, turning once, for 10 minutes or until golden and crisp. Set aside to cool slightly.

- Preheat a chargrill on high. Spray lightly with olive oil spray. Sprinkle the lamb with 2 teaspoons of dukkah. Cook on grill for 2 minutes each side for medium or until cooked to your liking. Transfer to a plate and cover with foil. Set aside for 2-3 minutes to rest.
- Break the bread into small pieces. Place in a large bowl. Add the cucumber, capsicum, shallot, parsley, mint and lemon juice. Season with pepper. Toss gently to combine.
- Divide the salad and lamb among serving plates. Sprinkle with the remaining dukkah to serve.

Nutrition Information

- Calories: 221.075 calories
- Total Carbohydrate: 17 grams carbohydrates
- Protein: 20 grams protein
- Total Fat: 7.5 grams fat
- Saturated Fat: 2.5 grams saturated fat

160. Portuguese Style BBQ Lamb Cutlets

Serving: 6 | Prep: 70mins | Ready in: 80mins

Ingredients

- 12 Coles Australian Lamb Cutlets
- 1/2 cup (125ml) red wine vinegar
- 1/3 cup (80ml) olive oil
- 1 1/2 tbs ground paprika
- 1 tbs brown sugar
- 1 tbs dried oregano
- 2 tsp thyme leaves
- 2 garlic cloves, crushed
- 1 long red chilli, seeded, finely chopped (optional)

Direction

- To make the marinade, place the vinegar, oil, paprika, sugar, oregano, thyme, garlic and chilli, if using, in a large bowl and stir until the sugar dissolves.
- Add 12 Coles Australian Lamb Cutlets to the marinade and turn to coat. Cover and place in the fridge for 1 hour.
- Heat a barbecue grill or chargrill on medium. Drain lamb, reserving 2 tbsp. of the marinade. Cook lamb for 1 min. Turn and brush cooked side with half the reserved marinade. Cook for 1 min. Repeat. Cook for a further 2 mins each side or until cooked to your liking. Set aside for 5 mins to rest. Sprinkle with thyme.

161. Quick Garlic Lamb With Chargrilled Pineapple Slaw

Serving: 4 | Prep: 15mins | Ready in: 25mins

Ingredients

- 1/4 pineapple, peeled, thinly sliced
- 1 tablespoon olive oil
- 1 garlic clove, crushed
- 12 Coles Australian Lamb Loin Chops
- 400g pkt Coles American BBQ Slaw Kit
- Lemon wedges, to serve

Direction

- Heat a barbecue grill or chargrill on high. Cook the pineapple for 1-2 mins each side or until charred. Transfer to a plate and set aside to cool.
- Combine the oil and garlic in a shallow glass or ceramic dish. Add lamb and turn to coat. Cook on grill for 3 mins each side or until cooked to your liking. Transfer to a plate. Cover and set aside for 5 mins to rest.
- Meanwhile, prepare the slaw kit in large bowl following packet directions. Add pineapple and toss to combine. Season.
- Serve lamb with slaw mixture and lemon wedges.

162. Quick Harissa Lamb Chops With Asparagus And Bean Salad

Serving: 4 | Prep: 20mins | Ready in: 30mins

Ingredients

- 250g green beans, ends trimmed
- 2 bunches asparagus, woody ends trimmed, halved
- 8 Coles Australian Lamb Loin Chops
- 1/4 cup (20g) flaked almonds, toasted
- 120g pkt Coles Australian Baby Rocket
- 200g beetroot dip
- 2 teaspoons ground cumin
- 1 teaspoon ground coriander
- 1 teaspoon smoked paprika
- 1 teaspoon caraway seeds
- 1 teaspoon garlic powder
- 1 teaspoon dried chilli flakes (optional)
- 200g Greek-style yoghurt
- 1/2 cup finely chopped mint

Direction

- Cook beans and asparagus in a large saucepan of boiling water for 2 mins or until bright green and tender crisp. Refresh under cold water. Drain well.
- To make the harissa spice mix, combine cumin, coriander, paprika, caraway seeds, garlic powder and chili, if using, in a bowl. Season.
- Heat a barbecue grill or chargrill on medium-high. Sprinkle the harissa spice mix evenly over the lamb. Cook on grill for 2-3 mins each side for medium or until cooked to your liking. Transfer to a plate and cover with foil. Set aside for 5 mins to rest.
- To make the minted yoghurt, combine yoghurt and mint in a bowl. Season. Add the almond and rocket to the bean mixture. Toss to combine. Divide bean salad and beetroot dip among serving plates. Top with the lamb and serve with minted yoghurt.

Nutrition Information

- Calories: 409.646 calories
- Sugar: 13 grams sugar
- Protein: 39 grams protein
- Total Fat: 19 grams fat
- Total Carbohydrate: 16 grams carbohydrates
- Saturated Fat: 7 grams saturated fat
- Sodium: 402 milligrams sodium

163. Roast Lamb Racks With Mixed Herb Labne

Serving: 6 | Prep: 500mins | Ready in: 520mins

Ingredients

- 260g (1 cup) pot-set low-fat Greek yoghurt
- 2 (400g each) French trimmed lamb racks (9 cutlets on each rack)
- 1/2 teaspoon ground sumac
- Pinch of salt
- 1 lemon, rind finely grated
- 1/4 cup fresh mint leaves, finely chopped
- 1/4 cup fresh continental parsley leaves, finely chopped
- 1 tablespoon finely chopped fresh chives
- Fresh mint, to serve
- Fresh continental parsley leaves, to serve
- Chopped fresh chives, to serve
- Lemon wedges, to serve

Direction

- For the labne, place a fine sieve over a bowl. Line the sieve with a double layer of muslin. Place the yoghurt in the center of the muslin. Bring the edges together to enclose and twist to secure. Place in the fridge for 8 hours or overnight to drain.

- Preheat oven to 180C/160C fan forced. Spray the lamb racks with olive oil. Sprinkle with the sumac and salt. Season with pepper. Heat a large non-stick frying pan over medium-high heat. Cook the lamb, turning, for 5 minutes or until browned. Transfer to a roasting pan. Roast for 12-14 minutes for medium or until cooked to your liking. Set aside to rest for 6 minutes.
- Meanwhile, remove the labne from the muslin and transfer to a clean bowl. Stir in the lemon rind, mint, parsley and chives. Season with pepper.
- Carve each rack into 3 portions. Arrange on a serving platter and sprinkle with mint, parsley, chives and pepper. Serve with labne and lemon wedges.

Nutrition Information

- Calories: 243.78 calories
- Total Fat: 11 grams fat
- Saturated Fat: 5 grams saturated fat
- Total Carbohydrate: 7 grams carbohydrates
- Protein: 28 grams protein
- Sodium: 83 milligrams sodium
- Sugar: 6 grams sugar

164. Rosemary And Chilli Lamb Chops With Chargrilled Polenta

Serving: 4 | Prep: 85mins | Ready in: 110mins

Ingredients

- 2 tablespoons fresh rosemary leaves
- 1 small fresh red chilli
- 1 garlic clove, coarsely chopped
- 2 tablespoons fresh lemon juice
- 2 tablespoons olive oil, plus extra to grease
- 4 Coles lamb loin chops
- 1 medium eggplant, halved lengthways, cut into 1cm-thick slices
- 2 zucchini, thickly sliced diagonally
- 750g ready to serve polenta (Romanella brand), squared off and cut into 8 slices
- 2 roma tomatoes, sliced
- 6 bocconcini, coarsely torn
- 1 tablespoon balsamic vinegar

Direction

- Process the rosemary, chilli, garlic, juice and half the oil in a stab mixer or hand blender (alternatively pound the rosemary, chilli and garlic in a mortar and pestle and stir in the juice and oil). Place the chops in a small dish and pour over the marinade. Place in the fridge for 1 hour or ideally overnight to marinate.
- Preheat a large barbecue plate or char-grill over medium-high heat. Grease with a little oil. Add the eggplant and zucchini. Cook the zucchini for 2 minutes each side and the eggplant for 4 minutes each side. Transfer to a large plate and cover with foil. Brush the polenta slices with a little oil. Cook for 3-4 minutes each side or until golden. Transfer to the plate with the vegetables.
- Remove the chops from the marinade. Season with salt and pepper. Cook for 2-3 minutes each side for medium or until cooked to your liking.
- Combine the vinegar with the remaining oil. Arrange the polenta, eggplant, zucchini and tomato on serving plates. Season with salt and pepper. Scatter with the bocconcini and drizzle with the dressing. Divide the chops between the plates.

Nutrition Information

- Calories: 664.181 calories
- Protein: 49.9 grams protein
- Sodium: 352 milligrams sodium
- Total Fat: 26.5 grams fat
- Total Carbohydrate: 56.7 grams carbohydrates
- Sugar: 7.4 grams sugar

- Saturated Fat: 11.1 grams saturated fat
- Cholesterol: 141 milligrams cholesterol

165. Rosemary And Garlic Lamb Chops

Serving: 4 | Prep: 0S | Ready in: 30mins

Ingredients

- 2 tablespoons orange juice
- 2 tablespoons Coles Brand Italian red wine vinegar
- 2 cloves garlic, crushed
- 2 teaspoons rosemary, finely chopped
- 1/4 cup olive oil
- 8 Coles lamb loin chops
- 2 zucchini, sliced diagonally
- 2 red capsicums, cut into thick strips
- 250g cherry tomatoes
- 60g mixed salad leaves, to serve

Direction

- Preheat barbecue grill or chargrill on medium-high. Combine the orange juice, vinegar, garlic, rosemary and half of the oil in a shallow glass or ceramic dish. Add the lamb chops and turn to coat. Set aside for 10 minutes to marinate.
- Meanwhile, combine the vegetables and remaining oil in a bowl. Cook, turning, for 8 minutes or until tender and browned. Transfer to a plate.
- Cook lamb chops on grill for 3 minutes each side for medium or until cooked to your liking. Season. Serve with vegetables and salad leaves.

166. Rosemary Lamb Chops With Quinoa Salad

Serving: 4 | Prep: 15mins | Ready in: 30mins

Ingredients

- 1 cups (200g) white quinoa
- 150g sugar snap peas, trimmed
- 1 bunch asparagus, trimmed, cut into 3cm lengths
- 2 tablespoons olive oil
- 2 tablespoons rosemary leaves
- 8 (about 1kg) Coles Australian lamb loin chops
- 2 carrots, peeled, cut into ribbons
- 2 spring onions, thinly sliced
- 1 long red chilli, thinly sliced
- 1/3 cup fresh mint leaves
- 2 tablespoons lemon juice
- 2 teaspoons lemon zest

Direction

- Cook quinoa in a saucepan of boiling salted water for 12 mins. Add sugar snaps and asparagus and cook for a further 2 mins or until vegetables and quinoa are tender. Drain. Rinse under cold water. Drain and set aside.
- Meanwhile, combine 1 tbsp. oil, rosemary and lamb in a bowl. Season with salt and pepper. Heat a large frying pan on medium-high heat. Cook lamb for 3 mins each side or until cooked to your liking. Rest, covered, for 5 mins.
- Place quinoa, sugar snaps, asparagus, carrot, spring onion, chilli, mint, lemon juice and remaining oil in a large bowl. Season with salt and pepper. Toss to combine. Serve lamb on quinoa salad. Top with lemon zest.

167. Rosemary Lamb Cutlets With Green Goddess Dressing

Serving: 4 | Prep: 20mins | Ready in: 30mins

Ingredients

- 1 tablespoon rosemary, finely chopped
- 2 teaspoons garlic salt
- 2 tablespoons extra virgin olive oil
- 250g vine ripened cherry tomatoes
- 2 bunches asparagus, trimmed, halved
- 12 Coles Australian Lamb Cutlets
- Flat-leaf parsley leaves, to serve
- 1 Coles Bakery Stone Baked White Sourdough Vienna Loaf, sliced, buttered
- 1 avocado, halved, stoned, peeled, chopped
- 2 tablespoons white wine vinegar
- 2 tablespoons flat-leaf parsley, chopped
- 1 tablespoon chives, chopped
- 1 garlic clove, coarsely chopped
- 2 teaspoons lemon juice
- 1/4 cup (60ml) extra virgin olive oil
- 1/4 cup (60g) light sour cream

Direction

- To make the green goddess dressing, process the avocado, vinegar, parsley, chives, garlic, lemon juice, oil and sour cream in a food processor until smooth. Season. Place in the fridge.
- Combine rosemary, garlic salt and oil in a large bowl. Add cherry tomatoes, asparagus and lamb and toss to coat. Season with pepper. Set aside for 10 mins for flavours to develop.
- Heat a chargrill or large frying pan on medium-high. Cook lamb for 2-3 mins each side or until cooked to your liking. Transfer to a plate and cover with foil. Set aside for 5 mins to rest.
- Meanwhile, cook tomatoes and asparagus, turning occasionally, for 4 mins until charred.
- Sprinkle lamb with parsley. Serve with salad, dressing and bread.

168. Rosemary, Lemon Seeded Mustard Lamb Cutlets

Serving: 44 | Prep: 15mins | Ready in: 55mins

Ingredients

- 60ml (1/4 cup) white wine
- 1 tablespoon wholegrain mustard
- 2 teaspoons chopped fresh rosemary
- 2 tablespoons fresh lemon juice
- 12 lamb cutlets, French trimmed
- 600g orange sweet potato (kumara), peeled, cut into 2cm pieces
- Olive oil spray
- 2 teaspoons olive oil
- 100g baby spinach leaves
- 1 small red onion, thinly sliced

Direction

- Whisk together the wine, mustard, rosemary and 1 tablespoon lemon juice in a glass or ceramic bowl. Add the lamb and turn to coat. Cover and place in the fridge for 30 minutes to marinate.
- Meanwhile, preheat oven to 200°C. Line a baking tray with non-stick baking paper. Place the sweet potato, in a single layer, on the lined tray. Lightly spray with olive oil spray. Season with pepper. Roast, turning once, for 30 minutes or until sweet potato is tender and golden.
- Preheat a barbecue grill or chargrill on high. Lightly spray both sides of the lamb with oil spray. Cook on grill for 2 minutes each side for medium or until cooked to your liking. Transfer to a plate and cover with foil. Set aside for 5 minutes to rest.
- Combine the oil and remaining lemon juice in a jug. Combine the sweet potato, spinach and onion in a bowl. Drizzle over dressing. Toss to combine.
- Divide the lamb and salad among serving plates. Serve immediately.

Nutrition Information

- Calories: 38.718 calories
- Total Fat: 2 grams fat
- Sodium: 19.71 milligrams sodium
- Saturated Fat: 1 grams saturated fat
- Total Carbohydrate: 2 grams carbohydrates
- Sugar: 1 grams sugar
- Protein: 3 grams protein
- Cholesterol: 11 milligrams cholesterol

169. Scorched Tikka Chops With Tomato And Carrot Salad

Serving: 4 | Prep: 30mins | Ready in: 45mins

Ingredients

- 100g (1/3 cup) tikka masala curry paste
- 90g (1/3 cup) Greek yoghurt
- 8 (about 1kg) lamb loin chops
- 2 large carrots, peeled into ribbons
- 350g mixed baby tomatoes, halved
- 2 green shallots, thinly sliced
- 1 lemon, halved
- 1 1/2 tablespoons coconut oil
- 1/2 teaspoon brown mustard seeds
- 1/2 teaspoon cumin seeds
- 1 garlic clove, crushed
- 1/2 cup fresh coriander leaves, firmly packed
- 4 roti or chapati bread, warmed, to serve

Direction

- Combine curry paste and yoghurt in a glass bowl. Add chops. Turn to coat. Place in the fridge for 30 minutes or overnight to marinate.
- Combine carrot, tomato and shallot in a heatproof bowl. Juice half the lemon. Cut remaining half into wedges. Heat the oil in a frying pan over medium-low heat. Add seeds and garlic. Cook, stirring, for 1-2 minutes. Remove from heat. Stir in lemon juice. Quickly pour over carrot mixture. Season. Set aside to develop the flavours.
- Preheat a chargrill over medium- high heat. Spray chops with oil. Cook, on a piece of baking paper, turning, for 6-8 minutes for medium or until cooked to your liking. Transfer to a plate. Rest for 3 minutes. 4 Add coriander to carrot mixture. Toss to combine. Serve salad with chops, bread and lemon wedges.

Nutrition Information

- Calories: 529.624 calories
- Saturated Fat: 15 grams saturated fat
- Total Carbohydrate: 24 grams carbohydrates
- Total Fat: 33 grams fat
- Protein: 31 grams protein

170. Seared Lamb Forequarter Chops With Braised Spring Greens

Serving: 4 | Prep: 20mins | Ready in: 40mins

Ingredients

- 1/3 cup olive oil
- 4 (250-300g each) Coles Australian lamb forequarter chops, at room temperature
- 3 (300g each) large globe artichokes, trimmed, hearts cut into eighths (see Notes)
- 3/4 cup chicken stock
- 4 spring onions, thinly sliced
- 2 cloves garlic, finely chopped
- 2 bunches asparagus, trimmed, cut into 3cm pieces
- 1 cup (120g) peas or sugar snap or snow peas
- 3 cups (60g) baby spinach, loosely packed
- 1/2 cup fresh basil leaves
- 1 tablespoon lemon zest
- 1 tablespoon lemon juice

Direction

- Heat a large heavy frying pan over medium-high heat. Season the chops with salt and pepper. Add 2 tablespoons of the oil to the pan, then add the chops and cook for about 3 minutes per side, or until golden brown and a thermometer inserted into the centre of a chop registers 60C. Set the chops aside to rest. Wipe out the pan.
- In a small saucepan, combine the artichokes and chicken stock. Bring to a simmer, cover, and cook for about 5 minutes, or until the artichokes are just cooked. Transfer the artichokes and cooking liquid to the frying pan that the lamb was cooked in. Add the spring onions, garlic, and remaining 2 tablespoons of oil. Bring to a simmer and cook for about 2 minutes, or until the onion softens slightly.
- Add the asparagus and peas and cook for about 2 minutes, or until the peas are heated through. Add the spinach and basil and cook for about 1 minute, or until the spinach is wilted and the asparagus is just tender. Stir in the lemon zest and juice. Season to taste with salt.
- Divide the vegetables among 4 dinner plates and top with the chops.

171. Slow Cooker Lamb Chops In Red Wine Sauce

Serving: 4 | Prep: 20mins | Ready in: 330mins

Ingredients

- 1 teaspoon olive oil
- 1kg lamb forequarter chops, trimmed
- 1 red onion, halved, thinly sliced
- 3 garlic cloves, thinly sliced
- 410g can chopped tomatoes with paste (see note)
- 1 cup dry red wine
- 5 sprigs fresh thyme
- 1 sprig fresh rosemary
- 1 1/2 cups risoni
- 100g low-fat feta, crumbled
- 1/3 cup chopped flat-leaf parsley leaves
- 2 teaspoons lemon zest
- Salt, to season

Direction

- Heat oil in large deep non-stick frying pan over medium-high heat. Season lamb with salt and pepper. Add half the lamb to pan. Cook for 2 to 3 minutes each side or until browned. Transfer to the bowl of a 5.5 litre slow cooker. Repeat with remaining lamb.
- Reduce heat to medium. Add onion. Cook, stirring often, for 5 minutes or until softened. Add garlic. Cook for 1 minute or until fragrant. Add tomatoes, wine, thyme and rosemary. Season with salt and pepper. Pour over the lamb. Cover with lid. Cook on low for 5 hours or until lamb is tender.
- Cook pasta in a large saucepan of boiling, salted water, following packet directions, until tender. Drain.
- Sprinkle lamb with feta, parsley and lemon zest. Serve with risoni.

Nutrition Information

- Calories: 691.427 calories
- Saturated Fat: 7.9 grams saturated fat
- Sodium: 530 milligrams sodium
- Total Fat: 22.3 grams fat
- Total Carbohydrate: 63.8 grams carbohydrates
- Protein: 46.5 grams protein
- Cholesterol: 95 milligrams cholesterol

172. Slow Roasted Tomato Feta Salad With Grilled Lamb

Serving: 4 | Prep: 20mins | Ready in: 75mins

Ingredients

- 700g roma tomatoes, quartered
- 1 teaspoon sweet paprika
- 1 teaspoon dried oregano leaves
- Olive oil spray
- 8 lamb cutlets, French trimmed
- 400g can no-added-salt chickpeas
- 55g (1/3 cup) pitted kalamata olives, halved lengthways
- 4 shallots, pale section only, thinly sliced
- 75g baby rocket leaves
- 1 tablespoon balsamic vinegar
- 2 teaspoons olive oil
- 60g low-fat feta, crumbled

Direction

- Preheat oven to 160°C. Line a large baking tray with baking paper. Place tomato, cut-side up, on prepared tray. Sprinkle with paprika and oregano. Spray with oil and season with pepper. Roast for 45 minutes or until soft.
- Preheat a chargrill or non-stick frying pan on high. Lightly spray the lamb with oil. Cook for 2-3 minutes each side for medium or until cooked to your liking. Transfer to a large plate. Cover with foil and set aside for 2 minutes to rest.
- Place the tomato, chickpeas, olive, shallot and rocket in a bowl. Drizzle with vinegar and oil. Toss to combine.
- Divide lamb and tomato mixture among serving plates. Top with feta.

Nutrition Information

- Calories: 334.6 calories
- Total Fat: 14 grams fat
- Saturated Fat: 4.5 grams saturated fat
- Total Carbohydrate: 25 grams carbohydrates
- Protein: 27 grams protein

173. Smoky Lamb Cutlets With Corn And Tomato Succotash

Serving: 4 | Prep: 10mins | Ready in: 30mins

Ingredients

- 8 lamb cutlets, trimmed
- 1/4 cup smoky barbecue sauce
- 1 small brown onion
- 150g green beans
- 400g punnet tomato medley
- 1 tablespoon extra virgin olive oil
- 2 garlic cloves, crushed
- 410g can corn kernels, drained
- 1/4 cup Massel chicken style liquid stock
- 1/2 cup fresh flat-leaf parsley leaves
- 1 teaspoon smoked paprika
- Extra fresh flat-leaf parsley leaves, to serve
- Lime wedges, to serve
- Crusty bread, to serve
- 25g butter, chopped

Direction

- Place lamb in a large shallow glass or ceramic dish. Pour over sauce. Turn to coat. Set aside for 10 minutes.
- Meanwhile, halve onion and cut into thin slices. Trim beans and cut in half. Slice tomatoes.
- Preheat a chargrill pan or barbecue grill on medium heat. Cook lamb for 3 to 4 minutes each side for medium, or until cooked to your liking.
- Meanwhile, heat oil in a large frying pan over medium-high heat. Add onion. Cook, stirring, for 5 minutes or until softened. Add garlic, corn and beans. Cook for 3 minutes or until beans are bright green and just tender. Add stock. Bring to a simmer. Simmer for 1 minute. Remove from heat.
- Add butter, parsley and tomato. Season with salt and pepper. Toss gently to combine. Sprinkle with paprika and extra parsley. Serve

succotash with lamb, lime wedges and crusty bread.

Nutrition Information

- Calories: 657.25 calories
- Total Fat: 35 grams fat
- Saturated Fat: 14.3 grams saturated fat
- Total Carbohydrate: 47 grams carbohydrates
- Protein: 36.4 grams protein
- Cholesterol: 92 milligrams cholesterol
- Sodium: 781 milligrams sodium

174. Spice Crusted Lamb Cutlets

Serving: 8 | Prep: 10mins | Ready in: 15mins

Ingredients

- 16 (about 700g) lamb cutlets, excess fat trimmed
- 3 garlic cloves, crushed
- 2 tablespoons fresh lemon juice
- 3 teaspoons honey
- 2 teaspoons finely grated fresh ginger
- 2 teaspoons ground cumin
- 1 teaspoon Masterfoods Ground Coriander
- 1/2 teaspoon ground cinnamon

Direction

- Place the lamb cutlets in a large glass or ceramic dish. Combine the garlic, lemon juice, honey, ginger, cumin, ground coriander and cinnamon in a small bowl.
- Pour the marinade over the lamb and rub to evenly coat. Cover with plastic wrap and place in the fridge for 2 hours to develop the flavors.
- Preheat a barbecue grill or chargrill on high. Reduce heat to medium. Add the lamb and cook for 2 minutes each side for medium-rare or until cooked to your liking.
- Transfer lamb cutlets to a serving platter. Cover with foil and set aside for 5 minutes to rest before serving.

Nutrition Information

- Calories: 103.965 calories
- Total Fat: 4.5 grams fat
- Saturated Fat: 2 grams saturated fat
- Total Carbohydrate: 3 grams carbohydrates
- Protein: 14 grams protein

175. Spiced BBQ Lamb Chops And Cos With Coriander Lime Crema

Serving: 4 | Prep: 15mins | Ready in: 25mins

Ingredients

- 1/2 cup (120g) sour cream
- 1 cup (loosely packed) fresh coriander leaves (about 15g)
- 1 lime, zest finely grated, juiced
- 1/2 teaspoon Mexican chilli powder
- 1/2 teaspoon garlic powder
- 1/2 teaspoon smoked paprika
- 8 lamb loin chops
- Olive oil, for brushing
- 2 heads baby cos lettuce, halved lengthways
- 1 small red onion, thinly sliced into rings
- 4 radishes, thinly sliced
- 1/4 cup pumpkin seeds, toasted
- 50g Danish fetta, crumbled

Direction

- Prepare barbecue cooking grate and hot plate for high heat. In small food processor, blend sour cream, coriander, lime zest and 1 1/2 tablespoon lime juice until smooth. Season with salt. Set coriander-lime cream aside.
- In small bowl, mix chili powder, garlic powder and smoked paprika with 1 teaspoon salt and

1/2 teaspoon pepper. Coat lamb with oil and season with spice mixture. Cook lamb fat side down on barbecue hot plate for 1 minute to render fat. Transfer to grate side and cook lamb for 2 to 3 mins per side or until char marks form and an instant-read thermometer inserted into center of lamb registers 54C. Transfer lamb to 4 plates.

- Brush cut sides of cos with oil and sprinkle with salt and pepper. Barbecue cos cut side down for about 3 mins, or until char marks form
- Spoon some cream on plates alongside lamb. Arrange cos atop cream and drizzle with more cream. Scatter onions and radishes over. Sprinkle pumpkin seeds and feta over and serve.

176. Spiced Lamb Chops With Warm Chickpea Capsicum Salad

Serving: 6 | Prep: 15mins | Ready in: 30mins

Ingredients

- 12 (about 900g) lamb loin chops
- 60ml (1/4 cup) fresh lemon juice
- 3 teaspoons ground cumin
- 1 1/2 teaspoons sweet paprika
- 2 x 420g cans chickpeas, rinsed, drained
- 1/2 cup drained coarsely chopped Sandhurst Char-Grilled Capsicum
- 60ml (1/4 cup) extra virgin olive oil
- 1 red onion, halved, thinly sliced
- 2 garlic cloves, crushed
- 2 tablespoons red wine vinegar
- 1 1/2 cups fresh continental parsley leaves

Direction

- Combine lemon juice, cumin and paprika in a glass or ceramic bowl. Add the lamb and set aside for 5 minutes to marinate.
- Preheat a chargrill on medium-high. Cook the lamb for 3-4 minutes each side for medium or until cooked to your liking. Transfer to a plate. Cover with foil and set aside for 5 minutes to rest.
- Combine the chickpeas and capsicum in a bowl. Heat the oil in a large frying pan over medium heat. Cook the onion, stirring often, for 3 minutes or until soft. Add the garlic and red wine vinegar. Cook for 1 minute or until aromatic. Pour over the chickpea mixture. Add the parsley and gently toss to combine. Divide the chickpea salad among serving plates. Top with the lamb chops.

Nutrition Information

- Calories: 511.46 calories
- Cholesterol: 84 milligrams cholesterol
- Total Fat: 34 grams fat
- Saturated Fat: 12 grams saturated fat
- Protein: 35 grams protein
- Sodium: 291.97 milligrams sodium
- Total Carbohydrate: 14 grams carbohydrates
- Sugar: 2 grams sugar

177. Spiced Lamb Cutlets With Chunky Veggie Salad

Serving: 0 | Prep: 5mins | Ready in: 30mins

Ingredients

- 2 bunches Dutch carrots, ends trimmed
- 500g pkt Coles Australian Diced Butternut Pumpkin
- 1 red onion, cut into wedges
- 2 tablespoons olive oil
- 400g can lentils, rinsed, drained
- 1/3 cup (25g) Coles Australian Flaked Almonds, toasted
- 1/2 cup mint leaves
- 1 lemon, zested, juiced
- 200g Greek-style yoghurt

- 2 tablespoons finely chopped dill
- 12 Coles Australian Lamb Cutlets
- 2 teaspoons Moroccan seasoning

Direction

- Preheat oven to 200C. Line a baking tray with baking paper. Place carrot, pumpkin and onion on the lined tray. Drizzle with 2 teaspoons of the oil. Season. Roast, turning occasionally, for 20-25 mins or until vegetables are tender.
- Meanwhile, combine the lentils, almond and mint in a large bowl. Drizzle with the lemon juice and remaining oil. Season.
- Combine the yoghurt and dill in a small bowl. Season.
- Sprinkle lamb evenly with Moroccan seasoning. Heat a large frying pan over medium-high heat. Cook lamb for 2 mins each side for medium or until cooked to your liking. Transfer to a plate and cover with foil. Set aside for 5 mins to rest.
- Add the pumpkin mixture to the lentil mixture. Toss to combine. Divide among serving plates. Top with lamb and yoghurt mixture. Sprinkle with lemon zest.

Nutrition Information

- Calories: 616.142 calories
- Total Carbohydrate: 39 grams carbohydrates
- Sugar: 21 grams sugar
- Protein: 36 grams protein
- Saturated Fat: 10 grams saturated fat
- Sodium: 278 milligrams sodium
- Total Fat: 33 grams fat

178. Spiced Lamb Cutlets With Garlic Tomato Salad

Serving: 4 | Prep: 15mins | Ready in: 30mins

Ingredients

- 2 teaspoons cumin seeds
- 1 teaspoon cracked black pepper
- 3 teaspoons ground paprika
- 4 garlic cloves, crushed
- 8 lamb cutlets, trimmed
- 1/3 cup olive oil
- 2 large rounds Lebanese bread
- olive oil cooking spray
- 4 ripe tomatoes, sliced into rounds
- 200g grape tomatoes, halved lengthways
- 1 bunch flat-leaf parsley, leaves roughly chopped
- 2 large lemons

Direction

- Combine cumin, pepper, 2 teaspoons paprika, half the garlic and salt on a large plate. Press cutlets into spice mixture to coat.
- Heat 2 tablespoons oil in a frying pan over medium heat. Cook cutlets, in batches, for 4 minutes each side for medium or until cooked to your liking. Transfer to a plate. Cover with foil.
- Meanwhile, preheat oven to 180°C. Place bread on a baking tray and spray lightly with oil. Sprinkle with remaining 1 teaspoon paprika. Bake for 5 minutes or until crisp. Break bread into pieces.
- Divide tomatoes between plates. Sprinkle with remaining garlic. Top with parsley and bread pieces. Juice 1 lemon and cut remaining lemon into wedges. Whisk together 1/4 cup lemon juice, remaining 2 tablespoons oil and salt and pepper. Drizzle over salad. Toss to combine. Serve cutlets with salad and lemon wedges.

Nutrition Information

- Calories: 556.153 calories
- Saturated Fat: 7 grams saturated fat
- Total Carbohydrate: 35 grams carbohydrates
- Cholesterol: 80 milligrams cholesterol
- Sodium: 335.54 milligrams sodium
- Total Fat: 31 grams fat
- Sugar: 8 grams sugar

- Protein: 31 grams protein

179. Spiced Lamb Cutlets With Mixed Lentil Salad

Serving: 6 | Prep: 15mins | Ready in: 65mins

Ingredients

- 105g (1/2 cup) green lentils
- 500g jap or kent pumpkin, deseeded, peeled, cut into 2cm cubes
- 60ml (1/4 cup) peanut oil
- 2 teaspoons ground cumin
- 2 teaspoons garam marsala
- 2 teaspoons ground coriander
- Salt freshly ground black pepper
- 115g (1/2 cup) red split lentils
- 1 x 500g pkt frozen broad beans
- 2 garlic cloves, crushed
- 4 round (22cm diameter) chapatti wraps (Patak's brand)
- 12 (about 470g) lamb cutlets, excess fat trimmed
- 1 x 400g can chickpeas, rinsed, drained
- 1 red capsicum, halved, deseeded, finely chopped
- 1/2 cup firmly packed chopped fresh mint
- 1/2 cup firmly packed chopped fresh coriander
- 1 small red onion, halved, finely chopped
- 60ml (1/4 cup) fresh lemon juice
- Natural yoghurt, to serve

Direction

- Preheat oven to 200°C. Cook green lentils in a saucepan of salted boiling water for 40 minutes or until tender. Refresh under cold water. Drain.
- Meanwhile, place pumpkin, 1 tablespoon of the oil, and half each of the cumin, garam marsala and coriander in an ovenproof baking dish. Season with salt and pepper and toss to coat. Cook in preheated oven, turning once, for 20 minutes. Set aside for 15 minutes to cool.
- While pumpkin is cooking, cook red lentils in a saucepan of salted boiling water for 12 minutes. Refresh under cold water. Drain. Cook broad beans according to packet directions. Refresh under cold water. Drain, remove skins and set aside.
- Preheat grill on medium-high. Combine remaining oil and garlic. Brush both sides of each chapatti with oil mixture and cook under preheated grill for 1 minute each side. Set aside.
- Place lamb, remaining cumin, garam marsala and coriander in a bowl. Season with salt and pepper and gently toss to coat. Heat a non-stick frying pan over high heat. Add half the lamb and cook for 3 minutes each side for medium or until cooked to your liking. Transfer to a plate and cover loosely with foil. Repeat with remaining lamb.
- Break chapattis into small pieces and place in a bowl with green and red lentils, broad beans, pumpkin, chickpeas, capsicum, mint, coriander, onion and lemon juice. Gently toss to combine. Taste and season with salt and pepper.
- Spoon the mixed lentil salad among plates. Top with the spiced lamb and serve with yoghurt.

Nutrition Information

- Calories: 463.421 calories
- Sugar: 8 grams sugar
- Protein: 31 grams protein
- Cholesterol: 52 milligrams cholesterol
- Sodium: 244.37 milligrams sodium
- Total Fat: 19 grams fat
- Saturated Fat: 5 grams saturated fat
- Total Carbohydrate: 36 grams carbohydrates

180. Spiced Lamb Cutlets With Peach Salad Recipe

Serving: 4 | Prep: 10mins | Ready in: 20mins

Ingredients

- 12 Coles Australian Lamb Cutlets
- 2 tsp smoked paprika
- 1 tsp cumin seeds, crushed
- 1 tsp fennel seeds, crushed
- 1/3 cup (80ml) olive oil
- 2 yellow peaches or nectarines, cut into wedges
- 1 bunch asparagus, woody ends trimmed
- 1 tbs sherry vinegar
- 1 tsp honey
- 2 tsp wholegrain mustard
- 120g pkt Coles Australian Baby Rocket
- 100g goat's cheese, crumbled
- 1/4 cup (40g) smoked almonds, coarsely chopped

Direction

- Combine the lamb, paprika, cumin and fennel in a large bowl with 1 tbsp. of the oil. Season.
- Heat a barbecue grill or chargrill on medium-high. Cook the lamb for 2 mins each side for medium or until the lamb is cooked to your liking. Transfer to a plate and cover with foil. Set aside for 5 mins to rest.
- Meanwhile, cook the peach or nectarine and asparagus on the grill for 1-2 mins each side or until tender. Transfer to a plate.
- Whisk the vinegar, honey, mustard and remaining oil in a small jug. Season.
- Arrange the rocket, asparagus and peach or nectarine on a large serving platter. Drizzle with half the dressing. Sprinkle with the goat's cheese and almond. Serve immediately with the lamb and remaining dressing.

Nutrition Information

- Calories: 606.582 calories
- Sugar: 8 grams sugar
- Protein: 31 grams protein
- Total Fat: 49 grams fat
- Sodium: 380 milligrams sodium
- Saturated Fat: 16 grams saturated fat
- Total Carbohydrate: 9 grams carbohydrates

181. Spicy Cajun Lamb Cutlets

Serving: 0 | Prep: 40mins | Ready in: 52mins

Ingredients

- 12 (750g total) lamb cutlets, trimmed
- 2 teaspoons garlic salt
- 2 teaspoons onion powder
- 2 teaspoons dried oregano
- 2 teaspoons sweet paprika
- 1/2 teaspoon cayenne pepper
- 1 cup dried panko breadcrumbs
- 1/4 cup plain flour
- 1 egg
- Vegetable oil, for shallow frying
- Lemon wedges, to serve

Direction

- Using your hand, gently flatten meat on each cutlet. Combine garlic salt, onion powder, oregano, paprika, cayenne pepper and breadcrumbs in a shallow dish. Season well with pepper. Place flour on a large plate. Whisk egg in a shallow bowl.
- Coat each cutlet in flour, shaking off excess. Dip in egg. Coat in breadcrumb mixture. Place on a plate. Cover with plastic wrap. Refrigerate for 20 minutes.
- Pour oil into a large frying pan to cover base. Heat over medium heat. Cook cutlets, in batches, for 3 minutes each side for medium or until cooked to your liking. Transfer to a plate lined with paper towel to drain. Arrange on a platter and serve with lemon wedges.

Nutrition Information

- Calories: 92.732 calories
- Protein: 6.6 grams protein
- Cholesterol: 25 milligrams cholesterol
- Sodium: 173 milligrams sodium
- Total Carbohydrate: 5 grams carbohydrates
- Total Fat: 5 grams fat
- Saturated Fat: 1.5 grams saturated fat

182. Spicy Dukkah Crusted Lamb With Cauliflower Salad

Serving: 4 | Prep: 10mins | Ready in: 30mins

Ingredients

- 4 Coles Australian Lamb Forequarter Chops
- 1 tablespoon Table of Plenty Spicy Dukkah
- Olive oil spray
- 600g cauliflower, cut into florets
- 1 medium carrot, cut into matchsticks
- 1 medium red capsicum, thinly sliced
- 1/2 cup coriander leaves
- 1/2 cup (50g) pepitas (pumpkin seeds), toasted
- 2 tablespoons lime juice

Direction

- Combine lamb and dukkah in a shallow dish. Turn to coat. Spray lamb with oil.
- Heat a barbecue grill or chargrill on medium-high. Cook lamb for 3-4 mins each side for medium or until cooked to your liking. Transfer to a plate. Cover with foil. Set aside for 5 mins to rest.
- Meanwhile, cook cauliflower on grill, turning occasionally, for 10 mins or until charred and tender.
- Combine cauliflower, carrot, capsicum, coriander, pepitas and lime juice in a large bowl. Season well. Divide salad and lamb among serving plates.

183. Spicy Lamb Cutlets

Serving: 0 | Prep: 30mins | Ready in: 40mins

Ingredients

- 1 tablespoon olive oil
- 1 teaspoon ground cumin
- 1 teaspoon ground coriander
- 1 garlic clove, crushed
- 12 Heart Smart Frenched lamb cutlets
- 1 cup thick Greek-style yoghurt
- 1 bunch coriander, leaves picked and chopped
- Salt and pepper, to season

Direction

- Combine olive oil, ground cumin, ground coriander and garlic clove. Place lamb cutlets in a dish and spread with the spice mix. Marinate.
- Combine thick Greek-style yoghurt and fresh coriander. Season with salt and pepper. Refrigerate.
- Heat a barbeque or chargrill pan on medium-high. Cook the cutlets for 2-3 minutes each side for medium. Cool slightly, then serve with the dip.

184. Sticky Honey Lamb With Carrot And Lentil Slaw Recipe

Serving: 4 | Prep: 20mins | Ready in: 25mins

Ingredients

- 2 teaspoons chopped fresh rosemary leaves
- 2 tablespoons balsamic vinegar
- 1 tablespoon honey
- 2 tablespoons fresh lemon juice
- 12 small French-trimmed lamb cutlets
- 1 tablespoon extra virgin olive oil
- 400g can lentils, rinsed, drained
- 300g pkt pre-shredded carrot
- 80g baby spinach, shredded

- 2 tablespoons currants
- Fresh basil leaves, to serve

Direction

- Combine the rosemary, balsamic, honey and 1 tbsp. lemon juice in a shallow dish. Add lamb and turn to coat. Cover and set aside for 10 minutes to marinate.
- Meanwhile, combine oil and remaining lemon juice in a large bowl. Add lentils, carrot, spinach and currants. Season then toss to combine.
- Lightly spray a large non-stick frying pan with oil. Heat over medium-high heat. Remove the lamb from the marinade, reserving marinade. Cook lamb for 2 minutes each side or until cooked to your liking. Transfer to a plate. Cover lamb loosely with foil. Set aside for 3 minutes to rest. Return pan to high heat. Add the reserved marinade. Simmer for 1 minute or until reduced and syrupy.
- Arrange the carrot and lentil slaw on a serving platter. Top with the lamb and basil. Drizzle over the sticky balsamic sauce to serve.

Nutrition Information

- Calories: 293.014 calories
- Protein: 20.5 grams protein
- Saturated Fat: 3.1 grams saturated fat
- Total Fat: 11.1 grams fat
- Total Carbohydrate: 24.3 grams carbohydrates

185. Sticky Lamb Chops With Chickpea Salad

Serving: 4 | Prep: 10mins | Ready in: 16mins

Ingredients

- 2 tablespoons honey
- 1/3 cup lemon juice
- 1/4 cup extra virgin olive oil
- 2 tablespoons MasterFoods® Moroccan Seasoning, plus extra 1 teaspoon
- 12 lamb cutlets, trimmed
- 400g can chickpeas, drained, rinsed
- 250g cherry tomatoes, halved
- 1 Lebanese cucumber, thinly sliced into ribbons
- 60g baby spinach
- 1 small red onion, cut into thin wedges
- 2 tablespoons chopped dry roasted almonds
- Lemon wedges, to serve

Direction

- Combine honey, 2 tablespoons lemon juice, 2 tablespoons oil and spice mix in a bowl. Add lamb. Turn to coat.
- Heat a chargrill pan over medium heat. Add lamb. Cook for 3 minutes each side for medium or until cooked to your liking. Transfer to a plate. Cover loosely with foil to rest.
- Meanwhile, combine chickpeas, tomato, cucumber, spinach, onion, remaining lemon juice, remaining oil and extra spice mix in a bowl. Serve lamb with salad and lemon wedges, sprinkled with almonds.

186. Sticky Lamb Cutlets With Tomato And Mint Salsa

Serving: 4 | Prep: 375mins | Ready in: 385mins

Ingredients

- 60ml (1/4 cup) kecap manis
- 1 tbs apple cider vinegar
- 2 garlic cloves, finely chopped
- 2 tsp finely chopped fresh ginger
- 2 tsp ground cumin
- 12 lamb cutlets
- 2 tomatoes, quartered, seeded, coarsely chopped
- 2 tbs chopped fresh mint
- 1 tbs lime juice

- 500g Uncle Ben's Express Brown Rice

Direction

- Combine the kecap manis, vinegar, garlic, ginger and cumin in a glass or ceramic bowl. Add the lamb and stir to coat. Cover and place in the fridge for 4 hours or overnight to marinate.
- Combine the tomato, mint and lime juice in a bowl. Season.
- Preheat a chargrill over medium-high heat. Spray with oil. Cook lamb for 2-3 minutes each side for medium or until cooked to your liking. Season.
- Prepare the rice following packet directions. Divide among plates. Top with lamb and tomato salsa.

187. Sticky Rosemary And Currant Glazed Lamb

Serving: 4 | Prep: 15mins | Ready in: 25mins

Ingredients

- 60ml (1/4 cup) good-quality balsamic vinegar
- 2 fresh rosemary sprigs, leaves stripped
- 2 tablespoons currants
- 1 garlic clove, crushed
- 5 teaspoons extra virgin olive oil
- 12 French trimmed lamb cutlets
- 150g (3/4 cup) couscous
- 1 small lemon, rind finely grated, juiced
- 160ml boiling water
- 200g green beans, trimmed, thinly sliced lengthways, blanched
- 2 green shallots, thinly sliced
- 2 tablespoons water

Direction

- Combine vinegar, rosemary leaves, currants, garlic and 1 tbsp. oil in a glass or ceramic bowl. Season. Add lamb. Turn to coat. Set aside for 10 minutes to marinate.
- Meanwhile, place the couscous, lemon rind and juice in a small heatproof bowl. Pour over boiling water and remaining oil. Season. Cover. Set aside for 5 minutes to absorb. Fluff with a fork. Add beans and shallot. Toss to combine. Divide among plates.
- Heat a non-stick frying pan over medium-high heat. Remove cutlets from marinade, reserving marinade. Cook cutlets for 2 minutes. Turn and cook for 1 minute. Add reserved marinade and water. Cook for a further 1-2 minutes or until slightly reduced. Serve cutlets on top of couscous mixture. Spoon over glaze.

Nutrition Information

- Calories: 408.451 calories
- Total Fat: 14 grams fat
- Saturated Fat: 4 grams saturated fat
- Total Carbohydrate: 39 grams carbohydrates
- Protein: 32 grams protein

188. Sumac Lamb Cutlets With Chickpeas And Pumpkin

Serving: 4 | Prep: 20mins | Ready in: 40mins

Ingredients

- 700g pkt diced butternut pumpkin
- 2 tablespoons olive oil
- 2 zucchini, ends trimmed, thinly sliced into ribbons
- 12 (about 1kg) Coles Australian lamb cutlets, French-trimmed
- 2 teaspoons sumac
- 2 teaspoons paprika
- 2 tablespoons white wine vinegar
- 1 teaspoon Dijon mustard
- 400g can chickpeas, rinsed, drained
- 100g baby rocket leaves
- 100g marinated feta, crumbled

- 1/2 cup (140g) Greek-style yoghurt
- 1 tablespoon lemon juice

Direction

- Preheat oven to 200C. Line a baking tray with baking paper. Place the pumpkin on the tray and drizzle with 2 tsp. of the oil. Season with salt and pepper. Toss to combine. Bake, turning occasionally, for 20 mins or until golden brown and tender.
- Meanwhile, preheat a chargrill on high. Brush zucchini with a little of the remaining oil. Cook for 1 min each side or until lightly charred.
- Combine the lamb cutlets, sumac and half the paprika in a large bowl. Season with salt and pepper. Cook the lamb on the chargrill for 2 mins each side for medium or until cooked to your liking. Transfer to a plate, cover with foil and set aside for 5 mins to rest.
- Combine the vinegar, mustard and remaining oil in a screw-top jar. Shake to combine. Combine the pumpkin, zucchini, chickpeas and rocket in a large bowl. Drizzle with dressing and toss to combine. Divide among serving plates and sprinkle with the feta.
- Combine the yoghurt, lemon juice and remaining paprika in a bowl. Serve salad with the cutlets and the yoghurt mixture.

Nutrition Information

- Calories: 329.82 calories
- Total Fat: 72 grams fat
- Total Carbohydrate: 69 grams carbohydrates
- Protein: 102 grams protein
- Saturated Fat: 27 grams saturated fat

189. Sumac Lamb With Cauliflower Fritters

Serving: 4 | Prep: 15mins | Ready in: 30mins

Ingredients

- 3/4 cup plain flour
- 1 teaspoon ground cumin
- 1/2 teaspoon ground turmeric
- 1/4 cup finely chopped fresh coriander leaves
- 1 egg, lightly beaten
- 1/2 medium cauliflower, finely chopped (see note)
- Olive oil cooking spray
- 8 (800g) lamb chump chops
- 1 teaspoon sumac
- Olive oil, for shallow frying
- 1 cup Greek-style yoghurt
- Baby rocket, to serve
- Cherry tomatoes, to serve

Direction

- Combine flour, cumin, turmeric and half the coriander in a bowl. Place egg and ¾ cup cold water in a jug. Whisk to combine. Gradually whisk egg mixture into flour mixture to form a smooth batter. Season with salt and pepper. Stir in cauliflower.
- Lightly spray a frying pan or chargrill pan with oil. Heat over medium-high heat. Sprinkle lamb with sumac. Season with salt and pepper. Cook lamb for 3 to 4 minutes each side, for medium, or until cooked to your liking. Transfer to a plate. Cover loosely with foil. Set aside for 5 minutes to rest. 3
- Meanwhile, add enough oil to a large, deep frying pan to come 1cm up side of pan. Heat over medium-high heat. Drop 1 level tablespoon of batter into pan. Repeat 3 more times. Cook fritters for 2 to 3 minutes each side or until golden and cooked through. Transfer to a plate lined with paper towel. Cover with foil to keep warm. Repeat with remaining batter.
- Combine yoghurt and remaining coriander in a small bowl. Serve lamb with fritters, yoghurt, rocket and tomatoes.

Nutrition Information

- Calories: 582.204 calories
- Saturated Fat: 12.2 grams saturated fat
- Cholesterol: 157 milligrams cholesterol
- Sodium: 335 milligrams sodium
- Total Fat: 33.9 grams fat
- Total Carbohydrate: 26.7 grams carbohydrates
- Protein: 42 grams protein

- Sugar: 3 grams sugar
- Protein: 35 grams protein
- Cholesterol: 84 milligrams cholesterol
- Sodium: 311.22 milligrams sodium
- Total Fat: 43 grams fat
- Saturated Fat: 13 grams saturated fat
- Total Carbohydrate: 26 grams carbohydrates

190. Sumac Lamb With Tomato Bread Salad

Serving: 4 | Prep: 20mins | Ready in: 30mins

Ingredients

- 1/3 cup extra-virgin olive oil
- 200g crusty Italian bread, cut into 2cm pieces
- 8 lamb loin chops
- 2 teaspoons sumac
- 250g cherry tomatoes, halved
- 1/2 cup fresh basil leaves, torn
- 1 tablespoon red wine vinegar

Direction

- Heat 1 tablespoon oil in a frying pan over medium-high heat. Cook bread, stirring, for 5 minutes or until golden and crisp. Transfer to a bowl.
- Place chops, 1 tablespoon remaining oil and sumac in a bowl. Season with salt and pepper. Toss to combine. Heat a barbecue plate or chargrill over medium-high heat. Cook chops for 4 minutes each side for medium or until cooked to your liking. Transfer to a plate. Cover with foil. Rest for 4 minutes.
- Meanwhile, add tomatoes and basil to bread. Drizzle with vinegar and remaining oil. Toss to combine. Stand for 3 minutes for flavours to develop. Serve chops with tomato mixture.

Nutrition Information

- Calories: 630.721 calories

191. Sweet Lamb Chops With Coleslaw And Corn

Serving: 4 | Prep: 40mins | Ready in: 65mins

Ingredients

- 2 tablespoons olive oil, divided
- 1/3 cup (80ml) maple syrup
- 1 orange, zested and juiced
- 2 tablespoons finely chopped rosemary
- 8 Coles Lamb Forequarter chops
- 4 corn cobs, husks and silks removed
- 1/4 cup (20g) finely grated parmesan
- 250g Coles Australian coleslaw mix
- 2 spring onions, thinly sliced
- 1/4 cup (75g) whole-egg mayonnaise
- Salt pepper, to season

Direction

- Combine 1 tbsp. oil, maple syrup, orange juice, orange zest, and rosemary in a large snap lock bag or shallow glass bowl. Season with salt pepper. Add the lamb chops, and turn to coat thoroughly. Set aside to marinate for 30 minutes.
- Meanwhile, preheat a barbeque or char-grill pan to medium. Lightly brush corn with remaining 1 tbsp. oil. Cook on the grill, turning, for approximately 12 minutes or until tender and slightly charred. Transfer to a serving dish. Sprinkle with parmesan and season with salt pepper.
- Adjust heat on barbeque or char-grill pan to medium-high, and cook chops for 3 to 4 minutes on each side, for medium-rare, or

until cooked to your liking, turning often so they do not burn. Set chops aside on a plate, cover loosely with foil, and rest for 5 minutes.
- Combine coleslaw mix, spring onion and mayonnaise in a medium bowl. Season. Serve with chops and corn.

192. T Rex Cutlets

Serving: 8 | Prep: 10mins | Ready in: 19mins

Ingredients

- 2 teaspoons lemon pepper
- 1 teaspoon dried oregano
- 1 teaspoon garlic powder
- 2 teaspoons olive oil
- 8 French-trimmed lamb cutlets
- Tamar Valley Greek Style Yoghurt, to serve

Direction

- Combine lemon pepper, oregano, garlic powder and oil in a shallow bowl. Add lamb. Turn to coat.
- Heat a chargrill over medium-high heat. Cook cutlets, in 2 batches, for 2 minutes each side for medium or until cooked to your liking. Cover loosely with foil. Set aside for 5 minutes to rest.
- Serve lamb with yoghurt.

Nutrition Information

- Calories: 127.626 calories
- Sodium: 193 milligrams sodium
- Saturated Fat: 2.7 grams saturated fat
- Total Carbohydrate: 2.1 grams carbohydrates
- Protein: 13.8 grams protein
- Cholesterol: 44 milligrams cholesterol
- Total Fat: 7.3 grams fat

193. Tandoori Cutlets With Beetroot Raita

Serving: 4 | Prep: 15mins | Ready in: 25mins

Ingredients

- 1/4 cup (80g) tandoori paste
- 1/4 cup (60g) natural yoghurt
- 2 teaspoons finely grated ginger
- 12 (about 800g) lamb cutlets
- 2 carrots, cut into ribbons
- 2 Lebanese cucumbers, cut into ribbons
- 1 tablespoon lemon juice
- 1 cup coriander leaves
- Steamed Basmati rice, to serve
- 2 teaspoons cumin seeds
- 1 teaspoon black mustard seeds
- 1 cup (250g) natural yoghurt
- 1 medium beetroot, peeled, coarsely grated
- 1/3 cup (35g) desiccated coconut

Direction

- Combine the tandoori paste, yoghurt and ginger in a large glass or ceramic bowl. Add the lamb and turn to coat in tandoori mixture. Cover with plastic wrap and place in the fridge for 1 hour to marinate.
- To make the beetroot raita, place the cumin and mustard seeds in a small frying pan over medium heat. Cook, tossing, for 1 minute or until aromatic. Combine the cumin and mustard seeds, yoghurt, beetroot and coconut in a small bowl. Taste and season with salt and pepper.
- Heat a large frying pan over medium-high heat. Add the lamb cutlets and cook for 2-3 minutes each side for medium or until cooked to your liking. Transfer to a plate and cover with foil. Set aside for 5 minutes to rest.
- Combine the carrot, cucumber, lemon juice and coriander leaves in a large bowl. Divide among serving plates. Top with lamb cutlets. Serve immediately with beetroot raita and steamed rice, if desired.

Nutrition Information

- Calories: 525.8 calories
- Protein: 45 grams protein
- Sodium: 902.22 milligrams sodium
- Total Fat: 32 grams fat
- Saturated Fat: 14 grams saturated fat
- Total Carbohydrate: 11 grams carbohydrates
- Sugar: 10 grams sugar
- Cholesterol: 147 milligrams cholesterol

194. Tandoori Lamb Cutlets With Cucumber Salad

Serving: 4 | Prep: 30mins | Ready in: 42mins

Ingredients

- 12 lamb cutlets
- 2 tablespoons gluten-free tandoori paste
- 2 tablespoons Greek Style Yoghurt
- 2 teaspoons cumin seeds
- 2 tablespoons mango chutney
- 1 tablespoon lemon juice
- 1 tablespoon olive oil
- 2 Lebanese cucumbers, thinly sliced lengthways
- 2 carrots, peeled, thinly sliced lengthways
- 1/2 cup mint leaves
- 1/2 cup coriander leaves
- Mini pappadums, to serve
- Steamed basmati rice, to serve

Direction

- Combine the lamb cutlets, tandoori paste and yoghurt in a large bowl. Cover with plastic wrap and place in the fridge for 30 minutes to marinate.
- Heat a chargrill pan over high heat. Add lamb and cook for 2 minutes each side or until cooked to your liking. Transfer to a plate and cover with foil. Set aside for 5 minutes to rest.
- Meanwhile, toast cumin seeds in a small saucepan over medium heat. Remove from heat. Add mango chutney, lemon juice and oil and stir to combine. Season with salt and pepper.
- Combine cucumber, carrot, mint and coriander in a large bowl. Drizzle with mango dressing and toss to combine. Divide among serving plates. Top with lamb cutlets. Serve immediately with mint papadums and basmati rice.

Nutrition Information

- Calories: 557.826 calories
- Cholesterol: 230 milligrams cholesterol
- Sodium: 274 milligrams sodium
- Protein: 73.3 grams protein
- Total Fat: 23 grams fat
- Saturated Fat: 7.3 grams saturated fat
- Total Carbohydrate: 10.8 grams carbohydrates
- Sugar: 4.6 grams sugar

195. Tandoori Lamb Cutlets With Cucumber Salad Recipe

Serving: 4 | Prep: 7mins | Ready in: 14mins

Ingredients

- 12 Coles Australian Lamb Cutlets
- 1/2 x 200g pkt Coles Tandoori Marinade
- 1/2 cup (140g) Greek-style yoghurt
- 250g pkt microwavable coconut rice
- 1/4 cup (80g) mango chutney
- 2 tbs lemon juice
- 1 tbs olive oil
- 2 Lebanese cucumbers, peeled into ribbons
- 1 red onion, halved, thinly sliced
- 4 radishes, thinly sliced
- Coriander leaves, to serve
- 75g pkt plain mini pappadums

Direction

- Place the lamb, tandoori marinade and yoghurt in a large bowl. Stir to combine.
- Heat a chargrill on medium-high. Cook the lamb for 2 mins each side for medium or until cooked to your liking. Transfer to a plate and cover with foil to keep warm.
- Meanwhile, heat the rice following packet directions. Transfer to a medium bowl. Cover to keep warm.
- Combine the mango chutney, lemon juice and oil in a jug. Season.
- Combine cucumber, onion and radish in a medium bowl. Add half the mango chutney mixture. Gently stir to combine.
- Arrange the cucumber mixture on a large serving platter. Top with the lamb. Sprinkle with the coriander. Serve with the rice, pappadums and remaining mango chutney mixture.

Nutrition Information

- Calories: 604.909 calories
- Protein: 32 grams protein
- Sodium: 902 milligrams sodium
- Total Fat: 31 grams fat
- Saturated Fat: 12 grams saturated fat
- Total Carbohydrate: 45 grams carbohydrates
- Sugar: 18 grams sugar

196. Tandoori Lamb Salad

Serving: 4 | Prep: 10mins | Ready in: 20mins

Ingredients

- 1 1/2 tablespoons tandoori paste
- 1 tablespoon lemon juice
- 1/4 cup natural yoghurt
- 8 midloin lamb chops
- 1/2 small red onion, sliced
- 250g cherry tomatoes, halved
- 75g baby spinach leaves
- 1 lebanese cucumber, sliced

Direction

- Place the tandoori paste, lemon juice, yoghurt and two tablespoons water in a large, non-metallic bowl. Trim the fatty tails from the lamb chops and discard. Add the chops to the marinade. Stir to coat well. Cover and refrigerate for 15 minutes.
- Heat an oven grill to high heat. Drain the lamb from the marinade and place on a grill tray lined with foil. Cook for 5 minutes each side or until cooked to your liking. Remove and set aside for a couple of minutes.
- Arrange the onion, tomatoes, spinach leaves and cucumber on serving plates and top with lamb chops. Serve with a squeeze of lemon juice and toasted pita bread if desired.

197. Teriyaki Lamb Cutlets

Serving: 4 | Prep: 5mins | Ready in: 9mins

Ingredients

- 1/4 cup (60ml) salt-reduced soy sauce
- 1/4 cup (60ml) peanut oil
- 1 small clove garlic, crushed
- 1/2 teaspoon finely grated ginger
- 1 teaspoon honey
- 8-12 lamb cutlets, trimmed

Direction

- Place the soy, peanut oil, garlic, ginger, honey, and a little cracked black pepper in a large non-metallic bowl and stir until combined. Add cutlets and toss to coat. Cover and refrigerate for 20 minutes.
- Heat a barbecue or stove-top grill to medium-high. Cook the cutlets for 1-2 minutes on each side or until cooked to your liking. Serve cutlets with salad or steamed vegetables.

Nutrition Information

- Calories: 411.558 calories
- Sodium: 636.9 milligrams sodium
- Total Carbohydrate: 2 grams carbohydrates
- Protein: 35 grams protein
- Cholesterol: 121 milligrams cholesterol
- Total Fat: 29 grams fat
- Saturated Fat: 9 grams saturated fat
- Sugar: 2 grams sugar

198. Teriyaki Lamb Cutlets With Stir Fried Greens

Serving: 4 | Prep: 15mins | Ready in: 25mins

Ingredients

- 8 lamb cutlets
- 80ml (1/3 cup) Teriyaki Marinade
- 1 bunch choy sum, stems and leaves separated
- 1 1/2 tablespoons vegetable oil
- 1 bunch broccolini, halved lengthways
- 2 garlic cloves, crushed
- 1 teaspoon grated fresh ginger
- 2 tablespoons water
- 3 shallots, trimmed, thinly sliced
- 2 tablespoons rice wine vinegar
- 1 teaspoon sesame oil
- Steamed rice, to serve

Direction

- Brush the lamb with 2 tablespoons of the marinade.
- Cut choy sum stems in half crossways. Shred the leaves.
- Heat 2 teaspoons of vegetable oil in a non-stick frying pan over medium-high heat. Cook lamb for 2 minutes each side for medium. Transfer to a plate and cover with foil to rest.
- Meanwhile, heat remaining vegetable oil in a wok. Stir-fry choy sum stems, broccolini, garlic and ginger for 1 minute. Add the water. Stir-fry for 2 minutes. Add the shallot, vinegar, sesame oil and remaining marinade. Toss until heated through. Serve lamb and greens with steamed rice.

Nutrition Information

- Calories: 332.688 calories
- Saturated Fat: 6 grams saturated fat
- Cholesterol: 80 milligrams cholesterol
- Sodium: 428.99 milligrams sodium
- Total Fat: 23 grams fat
- Total Carbohydrate: 3 grams carbohydrates
- Sugar: 3 grams sugar
- Protein: 27 grams protein

199. Thai Dressed Lamb Cutlets With Spring Salad

Serving: 4 | Prep: 15mins | Ready in: 25mins

Ingredients

- 8 Frenched lamb cutlets
- 100ml fresh lime juice (about 3 limes)
- 2 tablespoons fish sauce
- 2 tablespoons caster sugar
- 1 red chilli, finely chopped
- 2 garlic cloves, finely chopped
- 1 tablespoon fresh chopped coriander
- 2 carrots, peeled, cut into matchsticks
- 3 celery stick, cut into matchsticks
- 150g snow peas, trimmed, shredded
- Extra coriander sprigs, to serve

Direction

- Place the lamb cutlets in a large ceramic dish in a single layer. Whisk together the lime juice, fish sauce, sugar, chilli, garlic and coriander until the sugar dissolves. Pour half of the lime dressing over the lamb and turn to coat evenly. Cover with plastic wrap and refrigerate for 1/2 hour or until required.

- Heat a chargrill over a medium-high heat. Add the lamb, and cook for 3 minutes each side or until cooked to your liking.
- Combine the carrots, celery and snow peas in a large bowl. Add the extra coriander sprigs and remaining dressing and toss to coat. Serve with the warm lamb cutlets.

Nutrition Information

- Calories: 259.793 calories
- Total Carbohydrate: 13 grams carbohydrates
- Total Fat: 11 grams fat
- Saturated Fat: 4 grams saturated fat
- Sugar: 13 grams sugar
- Protein: 26 grams protein
- Cholesterol: 80 milligrams cholesterol
- Sodium: 1093.46 milligrams sodium

200. Yoghurt Marinated Lamb With Potato Mint Salad

Serving: 4 | Prep: 20mins | Ready in: 35mins

Ingredients

- 8 lamb cutlets, French trimmed
- 90g (1/3 cup) low-fat natural yoghurt
- 1 garlic clove, crushed
- 2 tablespoons fresh lemon juice
- 500g kipfler potatoes, peeled, cut into 1cm-thick slices
- 200g green beans, topped
- Olive oil spray
- 1 teaspoon olive oil
- 1/3 cup fresh mint leaves
- 1/3 cup fresh continental parsley leaves
- Lemon wedges, to serve

Direction

- Place the lamb cutlets in a shallow glass or ceramic dish. Combine the yoghurt, garlic and lemon juice in a small bowl. Pour the yoghurt mixture over the lamb and turn to evenly coat. Cover and place in the fridge for 20 minutes to marinate.
- Meanwhile, cook potato in a steamer basket over a saucepan of simmering water for 6-7 minutes or until tender.
- Cook beans in a medium saucepan of boiling water for 3-4 minutes or until bright green and tender crisp. Refresh under cold running water. Drain.
- Lightly spray a large frying pan with olive oil spray. Place over high heat. Add the lamb and cook for 1-2 minutes each side for medium or until cooked to your liking. Place the potato, beans and oil in a large bowl and toss until well combined. Taste and season with pepper. Add the mint and parsley to the potato mixture and gently toss until just combined. Divide the potato mixture among serving plates and top with lamb. Serve immediately with lemon wedges, if desired.

Nutrition Information

- Calories: 309.744 calories
- Total Carbohydrate: 19 grams carbohydrates
- Sugar: 4 grams sugar
- Total Fat: 12 grams fat
- Saturated Fat: 5 grams saturated fat
- Protein: 28 grams protein
- Cholesterol: 84 milligrams cholesterol
- Sodium: 104.94 milligrams sodium

201. Za'atar Lamb Cutlets With Carrot And Orange Salad

Serving: 4 | Prep: 15mins | Ready in: 25mins

Ingredients

- 1/4 cup (25g) za'atar*
- 1/2 cup (125ml) extra virgin olive oil
- 12 lamb cutlets
- 1 teaspoon cumin seeds

- 1/2 teaspoon sweet paprika
- 1/4 teaspoon chilli flakes
- 2 oranges
- 1/2 teaspoon honey
- 2 large carrots, peeled, cut into julienne
- 1/2 cup firmly packed flat-leaf parsley leaves
- Green salad, to serve

Direction

- Combine za'atar and half the oil in a bowl. Add cutlets and rub mixture into lamb then set aside.
- Place cumin, paprika and chilli in a dry frying pan and cook, stirring over low heat, for 1 minute or until fragrant. Transfer to a bowl. Using a citrus zester, remove orange rind in thin strips and add to bowl. With a sharp knife, cut away peel with white pith from oranges, then segment by cutting down either side of membrane to release segments. Squeeze juice from membranes over spice mixture then add honey and remaining oil. Season with salt and pepper; then mix well. Add orange segments, carrot and parsley and toss to combine.
- Preheat a char-grill pan or barbecue over medium-high and cook lamb cutlets for 3 minutes each side for medium-rare. Serve cutlets with carrot salad and a green salad.

Nutrition Information

- Calories: 604.67 calories
- Saturated Fat: 11 grams saturated fat
- Sugar: 10 grams sugar
- Protein: 36 grams protein
- Cholesterol: 121 milligrams cholesterol
- Sodium: 138.3 milligrams sodium
- Total Fat: 45 grams fat
- Total Carbohydrate: 11 grams carbohydrates

202. Za'atar Crusted Lamb Cutlets

Serving: 6 | Prep: 135mins | Ready in: 145mins

Ingredients

- 2 tablespoons finely chopped thyme
- 2 tablespoons sesame seeds
- 1 tablespoon sumac (see note)
- 18 (about 1.8kg) lamb cutlets, French trimmed

Direction

- Combine thyme, sesame seeds and sumac in a large glass or ceramic bowl. Add the lamb and gently toss until well combined. Cover with plastic wrap and place in the fridge for 2 hours to develop the flavors.
- Preheat a barbecue on high. Season lamb with salt and pepper. Cook on barbecue for 2 minutes each side for medium or until cooked to your liking. Transfer to a plate. Cover with foil and set aside for 5 minutes to rest. Serve on a platter.

Nutrition Information

- Calories: 494.969 calories
- Protein: 58 grams protein
- Total Fat: 29 grams fat
- Sodium: 187.96 milligrams sodium
- Saturated Fat: 11 grams saturated fat
- Total Carbohydrate: 1 grams carbohydrates
- Cholesterol: 201 milligrams cholesterol

Index

A

Almond 4,64,102

Artichoke 4,42

Asparagus 4,5,46,94

Avocado 3,5,20,71

B

Bacon 3,9

Baguette 71,72

Barbecue sauce 80

Basil 3,4,16,26,50,56,70

Basmati rice 28,29,39,111

Beans 3,4,9,33,52

Beetroot 3,4,5,6,27,54,63,68,77,83,87,111

Bran 14,16,19,22,26,34,70,85,96

Bread 6,81,110

Broccoli 3,5,7,65,83

Butter 3,4,16,28,50,102

C

Capsicum 4,6,66,102

Carrot 3,4,5,6,24,54,64,66,87,98,106,115

Cauliflower 5,6,71,86,106,109

Cheese 3,16

Cherry 109

Chickpea 3,4,5,6,28,55,67,85,88,102,107,108

Chilli 3,4,5,14,22,32,55,56,90,95

Chips 4,64

Chutney 3,4,23,37

Cinnamon 4,62

Coconut 3,4,5,15,21,60,80

Cola 60

Coleslaw 6,18,110

Coriander 3,6,8,17,24,80,101,112

Couscous 3,4,5,7,21,22,30,54,86,89,91

Cream 5,38,71

Crumble 3,5,10,15,43,58,83

Cucumber 5,6,76,92,112

Cumin 3,9,27,28

Curry 3,8

D

Dijon mustard 52,63,75,108

E

Egg 4,14,26,53,56,60

English mustard 9

F

Fat 4,7,8,9,10,11,12,14,15,16,17,18,19,20,21,23,24,25,27,28,29,30,31,33,34,35,36,37,38,39,40,41,42,43,44,45,46,47,48,49,50,51,52,53,54,56,57,58,59,60,61,62,63,64,65,66,67,68,69,70,71,72,73,74,75,76,77,78,79,80,81,82,83,85,86,87,88,89,90,92,93,94,95,96,98,99,100,101,102,103,104,105,106,107,108,109,110,111,112,113,114,115,116

Fennel 3,9,32

Feta 3,4,5,32,52,57,66,99

French dressing 25,30

Fresh coriander 28,78

Fruit 3,21,30

G

Garlic 3,5,6,19,33,93,96,103

Gin 3,8,22

Gravy 4,24,51

H

Harissa 4,5,45,94

Heart 106

Honey 4,6,38,106

K

Kale 4,5,68,71

King Edward 80

L

Lamb 1,3,4,5,6,7,8,9,10,11,12,13,14,15,16,17,18,19,20,21,22,23,24,25,26,27,28,29,30,31,32,33,34,35,36,37,38,39,40,41,42,43,44,45,46,47,48,49,50,51,52,53,54,55,56,57,58,59,60,61,62,63,64,65,66,67,68,69,70,71,72,73,74,75,76,77,78,79,80,81,82,83,84,85,86,87,88,89,90,91,92,93,94,95,96,97,98,99,100,101,102,103,104,105,106,107,108,109,110,112,113,114,115,116

Lemon 3,4,5,16,19,24,26,28,32,33,35,40,44,46,47,74,75,76,77,81,86,91,93,94,97,105,107,115

Lettuce 3,31

Lime 6,22,39,80,100,101

M

Macadamia 5,77

Mango 5,86

Meat 5,81

Mint 3,4,5,6,13,14,33,36,57,59,61,70,71,82,83,89,107,115

Mustard 5,89,97

N

Nut 3,7,8,9,10,11,12,14,15,17,18,20,21,23,24,25,27,28,29,30,31,33,34,35,36,37,38,39,40,41,42,43,44,45,46,47,48,49,50,51,52,53,54,56,57,58,59,60,61,62,63,64,65,66,67,68,69,70,71,72,73,74,75,76,77,78,79,80,81,82,83,85,86,87,88,89,90,92,93,94,95,98,99,100,101,102,103,104,105,107,108,109,110,111,112,113,114,115,116

O

Oil 16

Olive 3,4,11,14,16,28,35,36,39,44,52,54,55,62,63,69,70,78,83,91,92,97,100,101,106,109,115

Orange 3,5,6,22,90,115

Oregano 4,5,34,47,74,75,91

P

Parsley 5,75

Parsnip 4,64

Pasta 3,25

Peach 6,105

Pear 3,22

Peas 3,27,31,33

Peel 54,62

Pepper 3,4,5,19,68,85,91

Pesto 3,4,5,26,48,59,61,70,92

Pickle 4,56,66

Pineapple 5,93

Pistachio 4,61

Polenta 4,5,43,47,48,95

Port 5,81,93

Potato 3,4,5,6,12,27,37,38,42,48,59,69,79,80,82,89,115

Prosciutto 4,57

Pulse 87

Pumpkin 3,5,6,11,14,26,28,72,73,102,108

Q

Quinoa 3,4,5,24,41,85,96

R

Radish 3,4,5,29,62,87

Raita 6,111

Ratatouille 4,43,49

Rhubarb 5,91

Rice 3,4,5,7,15,29,40,60,84,86,108

Rocket 19,94,105

Rosemary 3,4,5,6,19,23,51,52,67,95,96,97,108

S

Salad 3,4,5,6,7,8,14,18,19,22,25,26,27,30,41,42,44,48,50,51,52,54,55,58,59,62,63,64,68,69,71,72,73,74,76,80,81,82,84,85,87,88,90,91,92,94,96,98,99,102,103,104,105,106,107,110,112,113,114,115

Salsa 3,4,6,13,14,55,65,66,107

Salt 29,63,85,99,104,106,110

Sea salt 51

Seasoning 107

Seeds 10

Spinach 3,4,8,19,30,39,67

Steak 5,71

Stew 4,39

Stock 54

Strawberry 4,41,52

Stuffing 4,45

Sugar 8,9,10,11,15,19,20,21,23,27,28,29,30,33,34,35,37,38,41,42,43,44,45,46,47,48,49,51,52,53,56,58,60,61,62,63,64,66,67,68,69,73,77,79,81,82,83,85,86,87,88,89,90,92,94,95,98,102,103,104,105,110,112,113,114,115,116

Sumac 3,6,27,108,109,110

T

Teriyaki 6,113,114

Thyme 5,75

Tomato 3,4,5,6,8,14,17,30,32,37,48,50,65,70,98,99,100,103,107,110

V

Vegetable oil 23,105

Vegetables 3,4,5,26,49,68,77

Vinegar 3,13

W

Watercress 4,59

Watermelon 3,8

Wine 3,4,5,13,67,99

Worcestershire sauce 40,80

Y

Yoghurt 3,4,6,29,31,39,45,62,90,111,112,115

Z

Zest 21,58,87

Conclusion

Thank you again for downloading this book!

I hope you enjoyed reading about my book!

If you enjoyed this book, please take the time to share your thoughts and post a review on Amazon. It'd be greatly appreciated!

Write me an honest review about the book – I truly value your opinion and thoughts and I will incorporate them into my next book, which is already underway.

Thank you!

If you have any questions, **feel free to contact at:** *author@smilecookbook.com*

Maria Howard

smilecookbook.com

www.ingramcontent.com/pod-product-compliance
Lightning Source LLC
Chambersburg PA
CBHW081122181224
19218CB00041B/571